CIRCLING TO THE CENTER

One Woman's Encounter with
Silent Prayer

Circling to the Center

One Woman's Encounter with Silent Prayer

Susan M. Tiberghien

PAULIST PRESS
New York / Mahwah, N.J.

Appreciation is due to the following publishers who have given me permission to quote passages from their books.

"The Lost Pearl," by Thomas Merton, from *The Way of Chuang Tzu*. Copyright © 1965 by the Abbey of Gethsemani. Reprinted by permission of New Directions Publishing Corp. and Gerald Pollinger, Ltd. "Legend of the Musk Deer," translated by Susan Tiberghien, from *Présence à Dieu, cent lettres sur la prière*, by Henri Caffarel. Copyright © 1960 by Editions du Feu Nouveau. Reprinted by permission of Danielle Waguet, Congregation St. Jean, Troussures. "The Sacred Hoop," from *Black Elk Speaks* by John G. Neihardt. Reprinted by permission of the University of Nebraska Press. Copyright © 1932, 1959, 1972 by John G. Neihardt. Copyright © 1961 by the John G. Neihardt Trust. "Tale of the Young Lover," translated by Susan Tiberghien, from *Présence à Dieu, cent lettres sur la prière*, by Henri Caffarel. Copyright © 1960 by Editions du Feu Nouveau. Reprinted by permission of Danielle Waguet, Congregation St. Jean, Troussures. "Dark Night," from the *Collected Works of St. John of the Cross*, translated by Kieran Kavanaugh and Otilio Rodriguez. Copyright © 1979, 1991 by the Washington Province of Discalced Carmelites. ICS Publications, 2131 Lincoln Road N.E., Washington, D.C. 20002. "In Silence," by Thomas Merton, *The Collected Poems of Thomas Merton*. Copyright © 1957 by the Abbey of Gethsemani. Reprinted by permission of New Directions Publishing Corp. and Search Press Ltd. Excerpts from The Jerusalem Bible, copyright © 1985, 1966 by Darton, Longman and Todd Ltd. and Doubleday, a division of Random House, Inc. and les Editions du Cerf. Reprinted by permission of the publishers. Psalms used in the text are taken from New Revised Standard Version of the Bible, copyright © 1989 by the Division of Christian Education of the National Council of the Churches of Christ in the U.S.A. Used by permission. All rights reserved. Susan M. Tiberghien's poem, "The Pear Tree," originally appeared in *The Prose Poem: An International Journal*, Vol. 4, 1995.

Cover Design by Kokopelli Design Studio

Type design by Casa Modica

Library of Congress Cataloging-in-Publication Data

Tiberghien, Susan M.
    Circling to the center : one woman's encounter with silent prayer / by Susan M. Tiberghien.
        p. cm.
    Includes bibliographical references (p.).
    ISBN 0-8091-3940-5 (alk. paper)
    1. Tiberghien, Susan M. 2. Contemplation. 3. Christian biography. I. Title.

BR1725.T55 A3 2000
248.3´4–dc21

00-062365

Published by Paulist Press
997 Macarthur Boulevard
Mahwah, New Jersey 07430

www.paulistpress.com

Printed and bound in the
United States of America

Contents

Illustrations / vi
Acknowledgments / vii
Foreword / ix
Introduction / 1

CHAPTER ONE: CINQUEFOIL / 5
Cinquefoil (Prose Poem) / 7
Story of the Lost Pearl / 25

CHAPTER TWO: CHERRY TREE / 27
Cherry Tree (Prose Poem) / 29
Legend of the Musk Deer / 47

CHAPTER THREE: PEAR TREE / 49
Pear Tree (Prose Poem) / 51
The Sacred Hoop / 68

CHAPTER FOUR: ACORN / 69
Acorn (Prose Poem) / 71
Tale of the Young Lover / 90

CHAPTER FIVE: GOLDEN FLOWER / 91
Golden Flower (Prose Poem) / 93
Prayer Mandala / 112

Notes / 115
Suggested Readings / 119
Index / 141

Illustrations

Cinquefoil in Author's Hand. Photo: Karen McDermott.   6

Nightmare, Black Hole. Monoprint: Susan Tiberghien.   21

Cherry Tree, Grand Saconnex. Photo: Susan Tiberghien.   28

Stone Well, Port Cros. Photo: Pierre-Yves Tiberghien.
(Courtesy of Daimon Verlag,
    publisher of *Looking for Gold.*)   33

Pear Tree. Photo of Van Gogh Painting:
    Karen McDermott.   50

Pear Tree, Grand Saconnex. Photo: Karen McDermott.   50

Church, Samoëns. Photo: Karen McDermott.   62

Acorn. Photo: Karen McDermott.   70

Water Jug. Photo: Karen McDermott.   79

Black Madonna of Monts Voirons.
    Photo: Karen McDermott.   85

Double Buttercup. Photo: Susan Tiberghien.   92

Mandala: Cinquefoil. Monoprint: Susan Tiberghien.   109

Mandala: Golden Flower. Monoprint: Susan Tiberghien.   111

Acknowledgments

I would like to express gratitude to the many people who have helped me along the path of prayer. To my mother and father, who nourished my faith and respected my longing for solitude. To Pierre-Yves, my husband, who has walked with me for over forty years. To my children, Pierre, Cécile, Catherine, Christopher, Lucie and Daniel, who have taught me faith and patience as they found their own paths. This, my family, has given me love tenfold.

Then to my friends, friends from many years back, friends from our years in the Teams of Our Lady, in America, France, Belgium, Italy, Switzerland, to Rosemary Enthoven, who knows what books to send me from the other side of the world, to Marie Claire Ducret, who also knows and who lives close by. To more recent friends who have kindly read this manuscript, to Kim Oldfelt Ekeus, with whom I've shared moments of silence, to Wallis Wilde Menozzi, my poet-friend living in Italy, to Karen McDermott, whose art work continues to inspire me, to Kristina Schellinski. And to so many others....

I wish to thank also my friends in the International Women's Writing Guild and its founder, Hannelore Hahn, who have given me encouragement and affirmation, and with whom each summer at the Skidmore Conference I have found inspiration.

And to the religious who have guided me, and always been there—often unknowing—when I needed them. To Jean de la Croix Kaelin, who welcomed me into the Catholic Church forty years ago and has guided me since. To Henri Caffarel and many of the chaplains of the Teams of Our Lady, with whom Pierre-Yves and I strengthened our shared spirituality. To Richard Frost, my "Jungian" priest, for his insight and wisdom, a holy person of few words. And to Bernard Sartorius, who accompanied me into deeper faith.

With special gratitude to the Monastic Sisters of Bethlehem—for over thirty years they have welcomed me to their monastery on top of the Voirons—to their liturgies and to their silence. To Sister Maia, who, before coming to France and to the Monastery of Bethlehem, held our youngest son in her arms in war-stricken Saigon and who ever since has held him and his family in her heart.

To early encounters with Raissa Maritain and John C. C. Wu, both of whom opened my eyes to grace, both of whom I have found again in my reading of Thomas Merton. And if I had the good fortune to know Raissa, it was because of my mother-in-law, Madeleine Tiberghien Toulemonde. It was also my mother-in-law who introduced me to Father Kaelin. This leads me back to her oldest son, Pierre-Yves, standing by my side. In love.

I wish also to return to my above-mentioned friend, Karen McDermott, who showed me how to do monographs and whose many photos bring life to my story, just as her camera brought a smile to the Black Madonna of the Voirons.

And it has been a joy to work with my editor, Joseph Scott, C.S.P., at Paulist Press. From the first reception of my manuscript, his attention and support have encouraged me.

Foreword

This is a beautiful book. An inviting book. It can be a great delight if we have the wisdom to allow the time to savor. There is much of a mother's love here, reminding us of our call, all of us, to mother the Christ within ourselves and in others.

This is an eclectic work. It takes courage to be able to enter into the beauty and wisdom of other traditions. We have to have a certain short sureness and confidence in the possession of our own tradition. Otherwise we might become dabblers. The chapters tell us of such a woman, a woman of sure faith and tender, compassionate love.

We walk with the author through many beautiful reflections of reality. Yet we are made to soon enough realize that words, images, feelings and aspirations are not enough. They do not satisfy. We are seeking something deeper, more real—the communion that takes place in silence. In spite of our proneness to want to prove our worth and even our being by activity, we want to move from active to passive prayer. We have finally realized we do not know how to pray as we ought and we want to let the Holy Spirit pray within us, the child's cry "Abba." We have only to "live each present moment as it comes." And then we will be "who we are meant to be," no longer seeking to prove ourselves by doing. We will be content to have our prayer be "a dark gazing into the simple being of God alone."

It is very difficult for us to be truly simple. We do not

speak here of the simplicity that comes from a lack but rather the simplicity that comes from a rich integration. It is very difficult for us to simply let everything go and be with God in the center. This is where the gentle invitation of this volume is especially valuable as a complement to Father Thomas Keating's more austere teaching that directs us immediately into the center. Susan shares with us a method that she has experientially developed, a method that she humbly affirms is but "an example of one way of prayer."

Probably few will be able or want to adapt this way in its entirety. But this well-presented sharing of a lived experience, enriched by insightful stories, will invite us to look more deeply into our own practice of prayer. It will invite us to appreciate more what we have and even perhaps invite us to adapt our prayer practice in one way or another.

I thank Susan for this beautiful sharing and pray that it may bear rich fruit in the lives of many.

Father M. Basil Pennington, o.c.s.o.

INTRODUCTION

I have often said that a person who wishes to begin a good life should be like a man who draws a circle. Let him get the center in the right place and keep it so, then the circumference will be good.

Meister Eckhart, Sayings

The seeds of my book were planted in the dark, back in my childhood, before my birth, and still further back centuries ago. There is a crack running through the creation, a fault line, separating us from our Creator. We are born with a longing for wholeness, a longing for "one-ness." It is this calling of prayer that I wanted to write about.

A calling of prayer, or of contemplation or meditation. I chose the simplest word—*prayer*. *Contemplation* carries with it perhaps a more evident allusion to silence. Yet in our contemporary world, the word seems to speak to an elite. I wished to use a simpler word. *Meditation* often evokes a sense of method, of mental discourse. I wished rather to write about a way. A way of prayer, a path of prayer. And I wanted to prune the word of its extra foliage—expository prayer, intercessory prayer, liturgical prayer and other definitions—and reach into the sap of all prayer.

Prayer is an awareness and very often a waiting. The sap of prayer is love, feeding the entire creation. A hug, an embrace. So has prayer been for me, a way to embrace the creation and the Creator. And a way to let the creation and the Creator embrace me. This path of prayer has taken me to both heights and depths. In midlife, stranded on a path overgrown with weeds, thickets and briars, I looked for bearings through writing. Short stories and personal essays marked the boundaries, but I needed to go deeper. I entered Jungian analysis, searching for light in the darkness, an experience that I chronicled in *Looking for Gold*.

Gold dust I found, as stillness resurfaced in my life. My path recircled through space and time to the one eternal source. Circles of prayer. Concentric rings. When I read Meister Eckhart's advice to the aspiring disciple, my plans for this memoir came together. I drew circles, a circle for each chapter, each time trying to get the center in the right place and to keep it there. The chapters begin with an image of nature, portrayed in a prose poem, and ripple outwards to the circumference. To amplify the chapters, which are rooted in my Judeo-Christian tradition, I include legends from other traditions—Taoist, Hindu, Sufi, Native American—underlining the oneness of humanity's search for the sacred. A oneness that illuminates the oneness of its source.

I worked back and forth from real experience to translation of its meaning into universal symbols. As I wrote about the cinquefoil, cherry tree, pear tree, acorn, double buttercup, the images revealed living symbols of my religious experience—mandalas, black holes, wells of water, the Eucharist, a cracked jug, the golden flower. Symbols that not only pointed to something else but that reflected in their own roundness an inner structure of the soul.

It is this same circular structure that informs the progression of the five chapters. In chapter 1, the cinquefoil in its utter lightness takes me first to the lightness of my father's ashes. Yet his seeds were planted deep, giving me a drive to success all through schooling, while at the same time a thirst for solitude. A thirst for the unknown that finally took me to Europe, to a French husband, to two more decades of trying to succeed. It was when I could not hold my father's ashes that I saw the futility of my striving. It was time to let go and enter the silence. Thomas Merton and Saint John of the Cross helped lead me into the dark center of my cinquefoil.

In chapter 2, the cherry tree in our front yard needed water, fresh water. So did our adopted son. So did I. Saint Teresa of Avila wrote at length about this source of fresh water, which is within us. I grew up along the Hudson. In Europe smaller rivers meandered through my life. But near midlife, the river was only a trickle. The rules, structures and creeds had dried out my faith. Then, in a blessed moment of synchronicity, I was introduced to C. G. Jung and to the correspondence between Jung's spiritual path and Saint Teresa's. My heart caught fire. My faith surged forth like a wave in the ocean.

The pear tree in chapter 3 showed me that beauty is in the seeing. The same tree can be anorexic or full of white blossoms, depending upon the seer. My mother-in-law and my daughter take me by the hand into the dark. When I flounder, the anonymous author of the fourteenth-century *Cloud of Unknowing* tells me to carry on there in the dark, wrestling with "this blind nothing." My way of prayer becomes a dark gazing.

In chapter 4, the acorn has lost its shell. My own mother has shed her depression. We have within us an imprint of our destiny. The acorn becomes an oak tree. I become who I am. But the shell has to crack. The apophatic way takes me deeper into the dark. I too must find the crack that lights the dark. This longing for darkness takes me into

Jungian analysis and on to the Black Madonna, who welcomed my brokenness.

Then, in chapter 5, the simple cinquefoil became the double buttercup, the flower that the dark stranger gave me in a dream. The flower is the golden flower of the ancient Chinese text on alchemy and meditation. Prayer has its own alchemy, seeking to find the gold in our ordinary lives. Day and night come together. Light and darkness. Julian of Norwich wrote of the "one-ing" of God and the soul. I return to the mandala. God is the center and also the circumference.

The universality of the symbol of the circle overwhelms. I dip willingly into our universal heritage—the collective unconscious as C. G. Jung defined it, the precious spiritual treasure chest of humanity. The Taoist story of the lost pearl, the Hindu legend of the musk deer, the Sufi tale of the young lover, Black Elk's vision of the sacred hoop—they circle around the same center. Standing where I am, held by my Judeo-Christian roots, I open my arms and link hands with all humankind around our God. Together we pray. Together we are. Together God is.

Susan Marquardt Tiberghien

CHAPTER ONE:
CINQUEFOIL

Concealed in the heart of all beings, lies the Atman, the Spirit, the Self smaller than the smallest atom, greater than the greatest space.

The Upanishads

Cleave a piece of wood, I am there. Lift up the stone and you will find me there.

The Gospel According to Thomas

And in this he showed me something small, no bigger than a hazelnut, lying in the palm of my hand....I thought that because of its littleness it would suddenly have fallen into nothing. And I was answered in my understanding: It lasts and always will because God loves it.

Julian of Norwich, The Revelations of Divine Love

There is a power in the soul that flows from the spirit and remains in the spirit and is wholly spiritual. In this power God is always verdant and blossoming in all the joy and honor that he is in himself.

Meister Eckhart, The Essential Sermons

I hold in the palm of my hand a minuscule yellow flower,
a cinquefoil. The five petals form a mandala....

Cinquefoil
(Prose Poem)

I hold in the palm of my hand a minuscule yellow flower, a cinquefoil. The five petals form a mandala around the inner circle of seeds. The seeds are dark, about a dozen of them on little threads. Its green leaves and stem are hidden. My gaze is drawn to the center then out again to each petal. The flower weighs nothing, as light as air. When I close my eyes, I no longer know whether it is in my hand or has fallen to the ground. It called to me from the side of the path in New York. It is the same flower that grows along my front path in Geneva.

My father's ashes were as light as air, scattered in the small courtyard. I could not hold them in my hand. They were scattered before my arrival. I entered the church and wept. Each tear tinted gold in the sunlight of the stained-glass windows. The stem of grief stretched through me. My father in each tear. His melanoma surrounded by moist earth. Tumor spots dark brown like seeds.

The stem is slender and pulls me to the ground. My father always said, "Go do it." But now the doing is toppling me over. The flower needs to rest its head. The petals curl and shrivel. My father's ashes are light, light as my yellow flower. But his seeds are planted deep.

Seeds of my father, "faith of our fathers." The words come streaming back. I grew up sitting next to my father, and my mother and older sister, in the fourth pew to the left, in the Congregational Church in Briarcliff Manor. The stained-glass windows filtered the light. "Faith of our fathers, living still." Riveted to my own father's presence, I listened to his voice. "Go do it." He taught me to swim before I could barely walk. And to dive from the board at the village pool, "Bend down. Put your hands together. Now dive." When it was time to go to school, he sent me off confident I should be first. So I skipped ahead, going away to boarding school at thirteen, to college at sixteen. He cheered when I applied for a fellowship for graduate studies. And when I sailed to France on *La Liberté*, the transatlantic steamer, he brought a bottle of champagne to the stateroom to toast his little girl. My mother was there, but I was always my father's little girl.

All along I was a loner—playing alone, climbing trees alone, looking at books alone, daydreaming alone. Yet I never felt lonely. For company, I summoned up another father, our Father in Heaven, and spent my days in his presence. Until the age of five, I lived on a farm, where my parents rented the top floor of the white square farmhouse set far back from the road, in the middle of fields. My father worked in New York City, my mother stayed at home and my older sister went to school. I played alone, mostly outside in the fields. I'd climb the log fences which reached out like spokes from the farmhouse, the center of my small world, to an ever widening circumference. I fed apples to the white horses that grazed every morning in the same field near the dark red barn, holding my palm as flat as I could, feeling the wet fat lips of the horse scoop up each apple.

And all day long, I kept company with God. He was there with me. Very early feelings of his presence were stored up in my memory like the autumn leaves my mother helped me wax and save in a scrapbook. I brought in handfuls of deep red oak leaves and dipped them in melted wax so that the color would linger through winter. Memories of playing in God's company dipped in wax.

Many years later, when I had children of this age, I rediscovered this same childlike confidence in God's presence in the words of a favorite psalm:

> O Lord, thou hast searched me and known me!
> Thou knowest when I sit down and when I rise up,
> Thou discernest my thoughts from afar....
> Whither shall I go from thy Spirit?
> Or whither shall I flee from thy presence?
> If I ascend to heaven thou are there!
> If I make my bed in Sheol, thou are there!
> If I take the wings of the morning
> and dwell in the uttermost parts of the sea,
> even there thy hand shall lead me,
> and thy right hand shall hold me.
>
> Psalm 139

I'd recite it with the children. "If we ascend up to heaven," and we'd raise our hands high above our heads to the heavens. Yes, the Lord would find us way up there. "Or if we descend down into the ground," we'd lower our hands to the earth. Yes, the Lord would be there too. "And if we take wings to fly away to the sea," and we'd wave our arms like birds. Still the Lord would be there. This was indeed how I felt growing up. The Lord was there.

When I was five we moved to a new house, all our own, on a dead-end road in a village called Briarcliff Manor. There were again fields beyond the road, and this time stone walls, old stone walls, and a hill covered with trees and bushes. Our house was one of five on one side of the road. Another set of five houses lined the other side. It never felt like the middle of my childhood world, as did the farmhouse in the middle of the fields. Instead I found my center place on top of the hill, above the white birch and pines, where there was a large rock half-embedded in the earth. In the sunlight the warm rock shone with glints of silver. I had to pull myself up the steep rocky ledge, fixing the toes of my sneakers onto the crack halfway up and hoisting myself to the top, where I would lie flat on my belly, very still and quiet. Then I would sit up and converse with the Lord God, telling him whatever was on my mind. My mother at home, my father working in New York City, my older sister with long dark wavy hair, my class at grade school, the swimming races, my broken arm, my one playmate who lived two houses down the road until she moved away, leaving me still more alone.

My grandmother on my mother's side came to live with us. She was sick and bedridden. One morning she didn't wake up. My parents didn't want me to see her dead, thinking I was too young at seven years old. I asked where she was. They said she had died. Would I see her again? What happened in death? What happened after death? Mother and Dad tried to quiet my fears. They said I shouldn't worry, that it would be like before I was born. But this didn't quiet my fears, fears fanned by her funeral and incineration, of which I kept a dreadful memory. A memory of her casket disappearing into a flaming furnace. Surely I did not see this. But in my child's imagination I did. And I saw the heavy iron dark door close behind the casket carrying my dead grandmother.

I went to my rock and cried out to God. The words of the Twenty-third Psalm from the King James Bible, "The Lord is my Shepherd," learned in Sunday School, came to my lips. "Yea, though I walk through the valley of the shadow of death, I will fear no evil: for thou art with me; thy rod and thy staff, they comfort me." I repeated the words over and over, again and again, until I felt comforted. During the night, when I was assailed with nightmares, I would put myself back on my rock, holding tight to his staff. "Thy rod and thy staff, they comfort me." Again, "Thy rod and thy staff, they comfort me." Until the words lulled me to sleep.

I grew up continuing to keep God company. I climbed into the trees, sat on my rock, walked to school, borrowed books from the library and set the table each night at home. I had my one friend, a girl my age, same short straight blond hair with a Dutch haircut. She lived two houses down the street. As we grew closer, I took her to my rock. We used to sit there together and share our stories and secrets. We used to talk about God. She didn't go to church and asked me why I did. Who is God? I tried to explain. How did I know? Because he kept me company. Because the sky was so blue. There was the song from Girl Scouts that asked why the sky's so blue. And the answer was that God made the sky so blue. We both knew the words. We'd sing it together. Then she moved away. Her parents were separating and sold the house. We cried. From then on Lord God was my only close friend.

When I entered tenth grade, I went off to the same boarding school my mother attended, the Hannah More

Academy in Maryland. I was still a loner. I appreciated the smaller classes, the smaller setting, the emphasis on learning. I loved the solitude of my little room in the middle of the sprawling red brick building. The school was high Episcopalian, and our days were punctuated with morning prayer and vespers. I was drawn into the liturgy and looked forward each Sunday to the ritual of the communion service, the candles and the incense, the long robes of the priest and the servers, the light and the shadows reflected on the cross, the symbolism of the bread and the wine, even though only confirmed Episcopalians were welcomed to the communion rail. I watched them kneel down and closed my eyes, imagining that I too knelt at the altar.

In my room, I spent long moments in prayer, kneeling at the side of my bed, my head in my hands. I was comfortable there. I would pray the Twenty-third Psalm and the Our Father, both of which connected me back to my Congregational upbringing. The prayers of the Episcopalian liturgy—the Sanctus, the Agnus Dei, the Kyrie Eleison—were not yet mine. I listened to them, in Latin, and the Kyrie in Greek, like passwords into a mystery that lay beyond my understanding. Whereas alone in my room, I felt at home and continued to pray the Our Father. It took up all my attention. I wanted to repeat the words straight through to the end without distraction. Whenever a daydream or an idle thought entered my mind, I would start again.

Gradually I stopped this exercise, this willful repetition of the entire prayer, and started to focus on the first line, "Our Father who art in heaven." Then just as gradually I focused only on the first words, "Our Father." I used it as a simple mantra, repeating it quietly, centering myself in the middle of my adolescent world. I'd repeat it aloud in my room, and I'd repeat it in my heart outside my room, going to class, going for a walk, back in the woods behind the hockey field. "Our Father." "Our Father." And soon only "Father." A single word. The simplicity of prayer.

Thomas Merton, the contemporary Cistercian monk, whose books have accompanied me all my adult life, wrote in one of his many journals about a single flower caught in a shaft of sunlight on the altar of the novitiate chapel at Gethsemani, his Trappist Abbey in Kentucky.

> This flower, this light, this moment, this silence: *Dominus est.* Eternity. He passes. He remains. We pass. In and out. He passes. We remain. We are nothing. We are everything. He is in us....The flower is itself. The light is itself. The silence is itself. I am myself.
>
> *Conjectures of a Guilty Bystander*[1]

Merton was writing here about the simplicity of prayer. This flower on the altar, in the shaft of light, *Dominus est.* The light is itself. The flower is itself.

I look at the golden cinquefoil in my hand. Five yellow petals, the number of completion. Quintessence—the essence of something in its purest form. The flower is complete in itself. It is God's gift. It is there in my hand yet I can hardly feel it. My father's ashes were scattered, as light as air. I was fifty years old when my father died. For thirty years I had lived in Europe, far away from him. But the dark seeds were planted deep. I was still striving to succeed, to go do it as my father used to say. I became Catholic, entering into the mystery of the liturgy that had captivated me as an adolescent, drawn still deeper into the symbolism of the Eucharist, in which God becomes man, so that man can become God, as imaged by Saint Irenaeus in the third century. I married a foreigner, the oldest son in a patriarchal, French family of ten children. And I moved to Europe, distancing myself from my family, from my friends, giving up my country, my culture, my language. French became my prayer language. I discovered that using a different language awakened the soul. Something mysterious happened that favored intuition over intellect. Somehow I could hear the word *Père* without the connotations that fluttered about the word *Father*, summoning up images of my father, of other fathers, of fathers in general. *Père* was a neutral word for me, lending itself more readily to transcendence. It was more inclusive and less gender limited. *Notre Père* (Our Father) embraced more easily for me all of creation. *Qui es au ciel* (Who art in heaven) spoke to me like poetry. I didn't try to think it through, to imagine where heaven was or what it was. Instead I held the words in my mouth and then in my heart. My personal prayer grew very simple, without frills, without extra words, a sincere yearning for the simple presence of God.

For twenty-five years I followed my husband, moving from country to country, raising six children in different places, different cultures, keeping our home open to family and friends. I tried to be both Mary and Martha, the two sisters whom Jesus loved and visited in the course of his journey—one sister sitting at his feet listening, the other busying herself with the house, the meal, the table. "Now Martha who was distracted with all the serving said, 'Lord, do you not care that my sister is leaving me to do the serving all by myself? Please tell her to help me.' But the Lord answered, 'Martha, Martha,' he said, 'you worry and fret about so many things, and few are needed, indeed only one. It is Mary who has chosen the better part; it is not to be taken from her'" (Luke 10:38-42). Only one thing was necessary. Mary had chosen the better part. And that part would be hers forever.

But during these many years it was Martha who won out. I took care of my husband and children, took care of my neighbors, took care of my friends, took care of whoever knocked on our front door. I volunteered at the different parishes where we lived, the different schools that the children attended, the different local associations. The story of Mary and Martha becomes very poignant in my memory, as I think back to an evening during our years in Italy. We had invited a highly esteemed theologian to our home for dinner, along with the members of our Team of Our Lady, a group of married couples, part of an international movement of spirituality. There were fifteen of us meeting in our living room and then around the dining room table. I cannot remember one thing this eminent priest said, but I remember still today the circle of chairs I arranged, the table cloth large enough to cover the bridge table too, the white plates I borrowed, even the veal marengo I prepared.

Ashes. As light as air. What does all this weigh? The stem bends, the petals curl. But this little yellow flower is loved by God. Faith. Not faith in words—dogmas and definitions—but faith without words. Faith in God's love, there in the middle of the farm, on the rock at the top of the hill, in my small room at boarding school. And at college, where I studied English and philosophy, reading T. S. Eliot and Henri Bergson. Faith in God's company wherever, whenever, everywhere, forever. A cinquefoil loved by God. A circle with dark seeds in the center. I grew up grounded in this space in the center. The petals of the flower reached out. Firmly rooted, I tried to hold the double tension of striving to achieve, while at the same time sitting still in my silent space.

What was this space? As a child it was a place to be with Lord God. A place where I could be myself. As I grew older, it was a place where I didn't have to excel. Where I didn't have to do anything. A place just to be. As an adult, the space moved with me, from America to France, not a cumbersome shell on my back, but rather something within, something warm and familiar, an essence, a source of rest and a source of strength. I sit still in this space. "Be still, and know that I am God," said the Lord (Psalm 46:10).

My roots reach deep into this ground of silence. This ground that Meister Eckhart, the medieval Dominican mystic, says is the birthing place of God, there where God speaks the Word in the midst of silence without ceasing.

> Here God enters the soul with his all, not merely with apart. God enters the ground of the soul....Now God needs no image and has no image....Thus it is and in no other way that God the Father gives birth to his Son in the ground and essence of the soul, and thus he unites himself with her.
>
> Sermon, "The Eternal Birth"[2]

This ground of silence was my space. It traveled with me, hidden in the innermost part of myself. Sometimes so hidden that I forgot it was there.

It was when I could not hold the ashes of my father that the slender stem started to bend over, the petals started to shrivel. What did it all matter? My father's ashes were scattered. I too would be scattered. My doings would shrivel. I would be as nothing. Only then could my heart be balanced in weight against the cinquefoil. When it would no longer be filled with references and definitions. No longer filled with achievements. No longer filled with attachments. No longer filled with family, with children and grandchildren. Emptied. Not even filled with husband and soul mate. When it would rest deep in the ground, there where there are no attachments, where there are no images. This is where I was gently being led. It was time to do less. Time to be more. To rest more. To rest in the hand of God, like the cinquefoil in my palm. Light, unattached, undemanding. The flower is. I am. God is. It was time to enter the center of the flower and sit in silence.

A way of prayer. To center ourselves in God. To dwell in the ground of our soul, where God mixes us with God's own very essence. Thomas Merton wrote volumes upon volumes about prayer, about contemplation. Like the yellow petals of my cinquefoil, I reach out and return to his books, wanting to widen forever the circumference. This is the familiar old pressure in me, wanting to understand, the habit holds on tight, its grip is strong and doesn't want to let go. I pull out a book and look for a reference. I turn the pages and reach for another book. I keep on looking. The stillness flees, the petals curl. But soon the dark center of the flower draws me back to silence. I am quiet. I listen.

Be still
Listen to the stones of the wall
Be silent, they try
To speak your
Name.

"In Silence," Thomas Merton[3]

The silence of prayer. The prayer of silence. Sitting in God's company. Finding our center and resting there.

Finding our *temenos*, the soft-sounding word that refers to the sacred space in and around the temple in ancient Greece. I draw my space around me and rest in my *temenos*. I sit there in the presence of God, remembering Mary, the sister who chose the better part, who sat at the feet of Jesus. Sometimes I sit there by sheer will power. Sometimes, much less often, I sit there by the grace of God, who pulls me still deeper into the center.

Merton described this way of prayer in a letter to Abdul Aziz, a Sufi scholar, with whom he had a long correspondence. The scholar asked him how he prayed. Although Merton rarely wrote directly about his own way of prayer, he replied to Aziz, who through letters had become his friend.

> I have a very simple way of prayer. It is centered entirely on attention to the presence of God and to His will and His love. That is to say that it is centered on faith by which alone we can know the presence of God....There is in my heart this great thirst to recognize totally the nothingness of all that is not God. My prayer is then a kind of praise rising up out of the center of Nothing and Silence.
>
> Letter to Abdul Aziz[4]

The center of Nothing and Silence. I look again at my cinquefoil. In the middle there is darkness. The center of nothing. Can I let myself fall into its dark center? Into nothing and silence?

I remember the dark tunnel that I first dreamed of as a child. It was during an operation, when I was three. I was going under ether when I entered a completely dark tunnel, a black hole, that went on endlessly. Unending darkness. Unending nothingness. When I awoke I was nauseous, my stomach wrenched. The black tunnel never completely disappeared. It huddled near me in the night. It came back with all its terror a few years later when again I was in the hospital, going under ether. I knew the dreaded darkness was approaching. I fought the ether. I fought its smell. I tried to push away the hands of the nurses and doctors. But they clamped the mask tight over my nose and mouth, and down I went. Falling, falling forever. A black tunnel, a black hole, a black nothingness, with no light whatsoever. There was no end to the darkness. No end to the tunnel.

From then on during the night, the dark hole often slinked around my bed. When it was upon me, I could not sleep. I would repeat the words, "The Lord is my shepherd...yea though I walk through the valley of the shadow of death, I will fear no evil; for thou art with me; thy rod and thy staff they comfort me." I would try to push the threatening darkness away. "I fear no evil for thou art with me...." I would get out of bed and walk around the room to try to shake it off. Still it threatened me, catching me off guard, overcoming me with angst. An eternity of nothingness.

Now at fifty years old, was I ready to enter the darkness? To let myself fall into the dark center? To enter willingly the dark tunnel? To lose myself—my belongings and my bearings—in its descent? To take off the masks I had carefully constructed, the controlled self I had fabricated? The mother striving to take care of everyone. The catechist at the parish, the parents' representative at the school, the volunteer at the youth center. To confront and peel away the layers of my exterior self?

I think of Inanna, in the ancient Sumerian legend written on clay tablets in the third millennium, the goddess of heaven and earth who went down into the earth's deepest ground to meet her sister, Eriskegal, the goddess of the

I entered a completely dark tunnel, a black hole that went on endlessly. Unending darkness. Unending nothingness.

underworld. As she went down, there were seven gates to pass. At each gate, Inanna had to shed one of her outer garments. Until she arrived empty and naked, without defense, in front of her fierce sister. Five thousand years ago, women were descending into their depths, abandoning all the false trappings and identities, to reclaim their darker half and discover their true selves.

Where was I? Holding on. Afraid to let go. Afraid of the dark. Always busy, unable to slow down, unable to stop. Always taking care of the needs of others. Unwilling to see myself as needy. Unwilling to let others see me as needy. Showing only my outer self, the self that was always in control. Hardly knowing my inner self. Afraid to find myself empty. Afraid to find nothing.

Thomas Merton speaks of the same journey in his book *Contemplative Prayer* when he writes that our true self is hidden in obscurity and nothingness, there at the center, where we are in direct dependence on God. We have to give up the self-important images of our mighty selves, the exaggerated estimates of our abilities, in order to sink into the deep ground of our identity in God and there lose ourselves in God's love.

> We should let ourselves be brought naked and
> defenseless into the center of that dread where we
> stand alone before God in our nothingness, without
> explanation, without theories, completely dependent
> upon his providential care, in dire need of the gift of
> his grace, his mercy and the light of faith.
>
> *Contemplative Prayer*[5]

My true self hidden away in darkness. Merton is clear. I should let myself be brought naked and defenseless before God.

The journey is ongoing. I take one small step. The darkness deepens. I lose my way and want to return. The ground is uneven. I stumble. Nothing is familiar. For a while I hesitate. Old doubts pull me backward. The way is too steep. There are no railings to grasp. I take another step. There is no light. I fall and hurt myself. Discouragement engulfs me. I pick myself up. Faith leads me on. It holds me by the hand even in the darkest of nights.

Here is the echo of Saint John of the Cross, the great medieval Spanish mystic, who spent a year imprisoned in the utter darkness of an underground cell. During the long months of solitary confinement, Saint John of the Cross had profound religious experiences that he expressed in superb poetry and prose. He writes that the way of the spiritual journey is like that of a blind man leaning only upon dark faith. The way is through darkness. "This dark night is an inflowing of God into the soul which purges it from its ignorances and imperfections."[6] He explains that this darkness is caused by the very presence of God. Our finite powers are blinded by the brightness of God's infinite being and truth. God's light is so radiant that only the man who sees by faith alone will find the way.

> One dark night,
> fired with love's urgent longings
> —ah, the sheer grace!—
> I went out unseen,
> my house being now all stilled...
> with no other light or guide
> than the one that burned in my heart.
> *The Dark Night*[7]

God brings us into the night so that in the darkness and without distraction—our house now stilled—we can see

the light that burns in our heart. Alone, with no one seeing us and with our seeing no one, the night welcomes our
journey.

I was to descend into the center of the cinquefoil, into
the ground of the little dark seeds. There where the seeds
become golden flowers. Where without belongings, having
left them behind, and without bearings, having lost them
all, I am led to the birth of my true self. This is the fertile
ground that Eckhart calls the "seedbed." It is the ground of
the soul. The place where God alone tills the soil, where
God waters the seeds of creation. The place within each of
us where God gives birth to the Son, where God's essence
unites with ours. *Ah, the sheer grace!* God's ground mixed
with our ground.

I sit in silence and close my eyes. I no longer know
whether the yellow cinquefoil—quintessence—is in my
palm or not. Slowly I let myself enter its dark center.

Story of the Lost Pearl

This story from Chuang Tzu, the Taoist master who wrote in the fourth century B.C., looks with shattering insight into the ground of being. The night-colored pearl represents the emperor's true nature, which in reality was never lost.

The Yellow Emperor went wandering
To the north of the Red Water
To the Kwan Lun mountain. He looked around
over the edge of the world. On the way home
He lost his night-colored pearl.

He sent out Science to seek his pearl, and got nothing.
He sent out Analysis to look for his pearl, and got nothing.
He sent out Logic to seek his pearl, and got nothing.
Then he asked Nothingness, and Nothingness had it!

The Yellow Emperor said,
"Strange, indeed. Nothingness
Who was not sent
Who did no work to find it
Had the night-colored pearl!"[8]

Chapter Two:
Cherry Tree

*Empty yourself of everything. Let the mind become still...
Returning to the source is stillness, which is the way of
nature.*

Lao Tsu, Tao Te Ching

*Prayer is the rippling tide of love which flows secretly
from God into the soul and draws it mightily back to its
Source.*
Mechthild of Magdeburg, Flowing Light of the Godhead

*Some nights stay up till dawn, as the moon sometimes
does for the sun. Be a full bucket pulled up the dark way
of a well, then lifted into light.*

Rumi (Jelaluddin of Konda), Poems

*God's love is like a river springing up in the depth of the
Divine Substance and flowing endlessly through His creation, filling all things with life and goodness and
strength.*

Thomas Merton, New Seeds of Contemplation

In our front yard there is an old cherry tree....
One spring several years ago it did not blossom.

Cherry Tree
(Prose Poem)

In our front yard, there is an old cherry tree. Its large trunk is covered with dark green ivy. For close to a century, it has born fruit. When I lean close against its ancient bark, it gives me strength. When I circle my arms around it, my hands do not touch. One spring, several years ago, it did not blossom. The summer before, there was not enough rain. The branches shriveled, the bark cracked. Sun scorched the ground. The roots of the cherry tree searched for a source of water.

Our youngest son was born in war-torn Vietnam. Sirens burst his ear drums. There was not enough nourishment. Hunger swelled his belly, polio twisted his leg. When he was two years old, he was buckled into a plane and flown away. At the airport in Geneva, his face was frozen with fear. His dark eyes looked for a familiar face.

That same spring I pulled out the garden hose and placed it at the foot of the old cherry tree. A pool of fresh water circled the trunk. It would take a while, but soon green leaves would come. In another year blossoms would appear, and then deep red cherries. I would leave the water on day after day.

I left the water on year after year. The old cherry tree needed a circle of water around its parched trunk. The tree now blossoms anew each spring. Its bark remains cracked, but its roots have found water. I left the water on also for our youngest son. Fresh water, like the water Jesus offered to the woman from Samaria, living water, "a spring of water welling up to eternal life" (John 4:14). Our son had survived the first two years of his life in war-torn Vietnam. His childhood in Switzerland, surrounded by brothers and sisters, helped him grow stronger. But adolescence knocked him down. He broke his right leg, then his right ankle, and then he broke it once again. He crashed his skis and smashed his tennis racquet. His souped-up moped was hauled away. He walked out of German class. The high school principal warned him once, warned him twice, then put him on probation.

He needed the faucet open. It wasn't easy. He was living in the basement, in the wine cellar we had fixed into a bedroom for his older brothers and sisters. Now they had all left home for university. Only our youngest remained. Like the cherry tree, the roots of our house needed water. Our son needed love, buckets of love, to heal the hurt and resentment that reached back to his earliest years. I was trying to write through the suffering. It was becoming a way of prayer. I sat in silence, asking God for love and strength, for my son, for me, for our family. Words formed slowly. I wrote them with tears.

"Give me a drink." Jesus is weary and alone, he sits down by an ancient well. A woman comes to draw water. Jesus asks her for a drink. She reproaches him, why does he, a Jew, ask her, a woman of Samaria, for a drink of water? Jesus replies that had she known the gift of God and who it was speaking to her, she would have instead asked him for water and he would have given her living water.

> Whoever drinks this water
> will get thirsty again;
> but anyone who drinks the water that I shall give
> will never be thirsty again:
> the water that I shall give
> will turn into a spring inside him, welling up to eternal life.
>
> John 4:13–14

I was asking God for living water. I needed to find the source of this water. A well of fresh water for my son. A well of fresh water for both of us and for the family. As I prayed, I would image a well of water. I had come across an old stone well on the island of Port Cros off the coast of southern France. The wall around it was broken, large stones had fallen to the side. I liked it still more. It was easier for me to lean into, easier for the water to flow out. A photo of the well sits on my shelf. I wrote about it. I prayed about it, imagining myself to be the cracked well, with a source of water deep within.

I remembered reading about a spring of fresh water in the teachings of Saint Teresa of Avila, the great Spanish mystic of the sixteenth century. It was in her book *The Interior Castle* that she gave instructions to the Carmelite novices about prayer. She told them to consider the soul as a castle with seven dwelling places, representing seven stages of prayer. As

An old stone well on the island of Port Cros....
The wall around it was broken....

the soul moves inward, from one circle to another, the way of prayer changes. In the first three circles, the soul practices active meditation. There is a well and the soul needs to work to pull up the water. Then in the fourth circle, there is a spring of fresh water. No longer does the soul need to draw the water. The spring overflows on its own as the soul moves into the last three circles, practicing passive meditation.

To illustrate the two different ways of meditation, Teresa gave the example of two water basins. One basin feeds the first three circles of her castle. The second basin feeds the last three circles.

> These two basins are filled with water in different ways: the water in the one comes from a long distance, by means of numerous conduits and through human skill, but the other has been constructed at the very source of the water and fills without making any noise....No skill is necessary here and no conduits have to be made for the water is flowing all the time.
>
> *The Interior Castle*[9]

If I follow Teresa in her interior castle, my meditation is active throughout the first three dwelling places. I must fetch the water, like the Samaritan woman, go to the well with my bucket, bend down to lower it, then pull it up and carry it back to my house. Here I must work at prayer. Each bucket of water is an effort. Whereas when I pass through the fourth dwelling place and enter the last three, my meditation becomes passive. The water in the spring bubbles up and overflows on its own. The bucket is no longer necessary. God lets loose the abundant spring and very soon the overflowing water becomes a sea, an immense ocean, and "with a powerful impulse, a huge wave rises up so forcefully that it lifts high this little bark that is our soul."[10]

I was praying for this huge wave. To lift up my son. To lift up my soul. I was writing in my journal trying to find my way through what was happening—his suffering and our suffering. I was making a space of silence in the little bedroom which had been his, where he had screamed his terror, night after night, upon his arrival. The walls no longer echoed his nightmares. From the window near my desk I could see the old cherry tree. I could see when it needed water. I was creating a *temenos*, where I could bring my heart and mind together, where I could write and pray in silence. A sacred space like the one in Saint Teresa's castle, where in the innermost chamber she meets her King, where her soul becomes one with its God. In this space, the wave would lift me and carry me on its curve.

It is here that the source overflows. It carries the Samaritan woman back to her village and family. She rushes to tell them about the person whom she has met at the fountain and who asked her for water. "The woman put down her water jar and hurried back to the town to tell the people, 'Come and see a man who has told me everything I ever did. I wonder if he is the Christ?'" (John 4:28-29). Likewise this bubbling source carries Teresa back outward to her Carmelite sisters in the many monasteries she founded. She has to show them how to build their own interior castles. "Oh, sisters! How shall I ever be able to tell you of the riches and the treasures and the delights which are to be found?"[11]

When the source overflows, it carries the soul with it. Our passive meditation reaches out to the world around us. For when we find this inner source deep within, contemplation becomes communion. God does not give his love to us alone to hoard up in our hearts. It would dry up and there would be no fruit. He gives it to us so that it overflows from our souls to other souls. His love is one movement, flowing inward and outward, forever. So it was that within this space, as I prayed in silence, not stopping to brush the tears away, I found buried deep within me a spring of water. My tears overflowed and slowly refreshed my heart. They joined the tears of my son. We held one another and cried. We listened to one another. We learned together to stand alone.

Imaging this source within me was not an entirely new experience. Water has always spoken to me. I grew up next to the Hudson River. Its vastness and its mighty currents were part of my childhood. From a hillside near my home, I would stare down at the flowing river, letting myself be carried along with it, moving onward, outward. When I traveled to France after university, my river continued to carry me outward, across the ocean. In Grenoble, where I was to study, there was another river, the Isère, winding through the city. It was smaller, quieter, and I felt the loss of the size and strength of the Hudson. My surroundings grew tamer. Gradually I adjusted to a quieter rhythm. The narrow winding river became a metaphor for my life in Europe, a meander moving, adapting, changing its course, making its path through the different countries in Europe where I lived and brought up children—France, Belgium, Italy, Switzerland. With time, I grew accustomed to its slower tempo.

During the early years of marriage we lived in Istres, a village in southern France built around an ancient church. I found time for quiet, time for living fully my first pregnancy. Here we joined our first Team of our Lady, an international movement of spirituality founded by Father Henri Caffarel in Paris in the 1940s, and met with other couples interested in finding ways to live their faith. The meander then ran northward to Brussels when Pierre accepted a position at the Commission of the Common Market, the embryo of the European Union. We settled into an old-fashioned apartment with a little courtyard, soon to be the playground for two more children. Welcomed by a Belgian Team, we made lasting friends and went on our first couples' retreats. After four years we moved to a small village in northern Italy, on a hillside above Lago Maggiore. With other couples, we helped to introduce the Teams to this part of Italy. Church bells kept time for us. Two more children were born.

The meander continued. We moved to Switzerland, to Geneva, finding a small house with bushes and trees enclosing a wide yard. The lake was not far away. It is here where we welcomed our son from Vietnam. With many friends from the Teams, we had started a prayer group in our home. The morning he was to arrive, we were to meet in the evening. His plane was delayed seven hours. When we came home from the airport with our new little son, our friends were there, praying in the living room.

Prayer steadied me during all those years. I prayed with my husband, prayed with our children, prayed with the parish, prayed with the Teams. These were vocal prayers, liturgical prayers, community prayers. For long periods, I went to daily Mass, drawn to the mystery of the incarnation—the divinization of the universe. There at the altar, wherever I was, I witnessed this ongoing divinization, which Teilhard de Chardin so beautifully rendered in his "The Mass on the World." It was in the steppes of Asia in 1923 that Teilhard celebrated his Mass, making the whole earth his altar and offering to God the labors and sufferings of the entire world.

> Once upon a time men took into your temple the first
> fruits of their harvests, the flower of their flocks. But
> the offering you mysteriously need every day to
> appease your hunger, to slake your thirst is nothing
> less than the growth of the world borne ever onwards
> in the stream of universal becoming.
>
> "The Mass on the World"[12]

There was also my personal prayer life, which had very
deep moments during and after each new birth. The time
of pregnancy, of this tangible inner growth, and then of
birth, awakened me to the cycle and miracle of all creation.
I was part of it. I welcomed each pregnancy with thanksgiving. To feel life within me, to feel this new life growing
in my womb, little hands and feet tapping from within,
this is extraordinary. Then the births. I entered into each
one of them, feeling the crescendo of pain until it became
so strong I felt I would not survive. In a way, I saw it like
death. Followed by the explosion of life. Life is stronger
than death. A baby, new and complete. A baby at my
breast. Milk flowed. Prayer came easily.

As we traveled, I looked for a center, a hearth, in each
new home. There are nomadic people who carry their center with them. In Australia, the Arunta tribe believed that a
pole cut from the highest tree was the center of their
world. As they moved across their vast continent, they carried their pole with them. Each time they set up a new
dwelling place, they planted the pole in the middle of their
tents. One day the pole disappeared. The whole tribe lay
down and died. I did not carry a pole with me, but in each
new dwelling I looked for a center. Most always it was the
dining room table, oval and large, with freshly cut flowers

arranged in a pewter vase in the center. In this way, I was lighting the fire in the hearth.

During these years Pierre was an important part of my prayer life. At Grenoble when we met as students, I shared with him my thirst for a deeper spirituality. When I returned to New York, we decided to read a book together, across the ocean. We chose *The Seven Storey Mountain*, the popular autobiography of Thomas Merton, relating his conversion and entrance into the Trappist Monastery at Gethsemani. The pages foreshadowed what soon would be my experience.

> I took up the book about Gerard Manley Hopkins. He was thinking of becoming a Catholic....All of a sudden, something began to stir within me, something began to push me, to prompt me. It was a movement that spoke like a voice. "What are you waiting for?" it said....I could bear it no longer. I put down the book, and got into my raincoat, and started down the stairs, out into the street.
>
> *The Seven Storey Mountain*[13]

There was much for us to discover in each other's way of seeing God. I was inquisitive, intuitive, impulsive. Pierre was more rational and structured, with generations of Catholic upbringing behind him. I questioned his traditional faith. He listened as I sought to define my own. When the Dominican priest, Father Kaelin, welcomed me into the Catholic Church, at Samoëns in the French Alps, Pierre was at my side. But never did he intrude. And as I continued to read voraciously—Saint Teresa of Avila, Saint John of the Cross, Teilhard de Chardin, Jacques and also Raissa Maritain, Jacques Loew, R. Voillaume, Karl Rahner—he remained a keen and grand listener.

In the early years of our marriage, the Teams of Our Lady helped us define our roles as husband and wife, as parents, and as married Christians. Coming from such different backgrounds, we needed to find our own way, neither American nor French, but rather bridging the two. We prayed together, sharing our intentions. As the children grew up, we continued to pray together as a family. The Teams were schools of spirituality for us, helping us to deepen our faith, to acquire the habit of prayer, to discover the silence of retreats and giving us lasting friends.

When we moved to Geneva, we were again close to Father Kaelin, who was continuing to guide my steps in faith. Now he helped guide our prayer group. He knew us both well. He especially knew my deep longing for silence and for solitude. This was not easy to satisfy. How does a mother leave and take off on her own? Could she imagine a hermitage in the backyard, following the example of Saint Nicolas de Flue, the Swiss saint, who left his wife and ten grown children to live and pray in a small hut not far from his house? Instead I would drive up to the nearby monastery on top of Mont Voirons, a holy mountain from Roman times, now the home of the Monastic Sisters of Bethlehem, looking for quiet, for an afternoon, a day, sometimes a weekend. Then I would hurry back to take care of the family, to fix dinner for the children and for Pierre, who was more and more caught up in the world of business. He was the provider. He looked toward me for keeping the river of God's peace flowing through our home.

But as I neared midlife, the river was becoming a stream, a trickle. The powerful waves were few and far between. My prayer life was stranded. I was rowing upstream. I think today of the words, *"Row, row, row your boat*, gently down the stream." It's a good song. Down the stream, not up the stream. And gently. A song I never understood when I was singing it with my own children. Only now do I listen carefully to the words when I sing it with my grandchildren. There I was, close to fifty years old, losing heart in private prayer. At church, my mind could no longer grasp the words of the prayers. Still less the words of the creed. I remained very much Martha, busy about keeping my house in order, but I was no longer trying to be Mary. I did not even miss sitting at the feet of Our Lord.

Then in one of those superb moments of synchronicity— those meaningful coincidences that defy all rational explanation—I received the book *Spiritual Pilgrims*, written by a Carmelite, John Welch, comparing the spiritual paths of Teresa of Avila and Carl Jung. The book was sent to me by a friend in California who knew it was the right book for me at that particular moment. It arrived when I was attending a lecture series on Carl Jung's spirituality, given by our parish priest. As the talks progressed, a spark ignited in my heart. I remember the disciples of Emmaus who, when they were returning home from Jerusalem, downcast and utterly abject after the crucifixion, were suddenly transformed. A stranger catches up with them and explains to them what has happened, scolding them for being so slow to believe. He stops at their house and breaks bread with them. Their eyes are opened and they recognize him, but he vanishes from their sight. "Did not our hearts burn within us," they said to one another, "as he talked to us on the road and explained the scriptures to us?" (Luke 24:31–32).

I was there, in the church, listening to our priest explain Jung's understanding of God, when a fire was lit in my heart. My rational doubts and hesitations went up in smoke. My tepid faith, which had become that of the indifferent believer whom God will spit out at the end of time, was rekindled. I was in front of the flaming bush. I wanted to take off my shoes. It was sacred ground. God was this fire, this numinous presence. God was within me. I was sacred ground. God was within the entire creation. The entire creation was sacred ground.

I went home and my friend's book was waiting for me. I plunged into it, refreshing my earlier reading of Saint Teresa, learning more about Jung and being in a very deep way reborn. Inflamed and immersed at the same time, fire and water, both signs of rebirth. The water of baptism along the sides of the Jordan River. Flames of the Spirit on the heads of the disciples at Pentecost. And when Nicodemus, one of the leading Pharisees, went in the middle of the night to talk to Jesus in Jerusalem, Jesus answered him, "I tell you most solemnly, unless a man is born through water and the Spirit, he cannot enter the Kingdom of God" (John 3:5).

Just as Teresa used water to image the presence of God, likewise Carl Jung, five centuries later, used water as a symbol for the inner depths of our being, the unknown part of the human soul. Even as a child, Jung was deeply affected by the magnitude of water, by the immense pleasure it gave him. As an adult he felt it necessary for his well-being to always live near a lake. It was through water that he felt restored, that he found his true self. Jung was imaging here the realm of the unconscious where consciousness originates. He called this realm the collective unconscious. It is our common source. Here is the home of the soul, the medium for union with God.

I remember hurrying out of the house and down to the parish, hoping to see our priest, wanting to speak of this water that was pouring out and setting me on fire. I rushed down the streets, feeling myself carried by an immense river. I wanted to exclaim to the priest that I had found the way, found my way back to God. That this collective unconscious bringing together all the spiritual traditions from around the world, throughout the centuries, was like a vast river coursing through the entire universe, giving rise to a forever new creation.

I rang the bell at the parish house. Father Richard Frost opened the door. He was on his way out. I said I'd be brief. I had only two questions. We stood at the doorway.

I started, "This collective unconscious that Jung identified, this immense creative current, could it not be an image for the Creator God?"

He nodded. "Yes, it could."

I dared to continue, "Then, could it not be that God incarnates in each of us, as indeed God fully did in Christ?"

He nodded again. "Yes, it could be so."

I had found my way. I was rushing with this inner current, I was spouting into the sky along with millions and millions of other water spouts all over the world. No longer was I meandering, brushing up against the shores of lukewarm liturgies, of dogmatic creeds, of patriarchal stances on doctrine. This was irrelevant. God was alive within all creation. God was alive within me. I was the broken well. The source was overflowing. Without water, my soul had dried up. The discovery of Carl Jung, along with Saint Teresa, both spiritual pilgrims, had uncovered the spring.

Without water, the old cherry tree had refused to blossom. I return now to its shade, lean against its ancient trunk. Round like the fountain in Samaria, like the old stone fountain in Port Cros. Round like Teresa's interior castle. Symbols of wholeness. Within the tree, the fountain, the castle, there is in the center, a source of water welling up into eternal life. Each of these mandala images focuses on the center. It is the center that gives them life. So in prayer I focus on the center. Prayer is itself a mandala. A mandala where in its innermost center, God gently leads us to Godself.

When I was a child I had two recurrent dreams. The first one depicted the dark tunnel—the black hole—threatening to engulf me, the dream that haunted me and that I wrote about in the first chapter. The second was instead a very pleasant dream that I often summoned back during the day, reliving it in my imagination. In this dream I was living in a round room, like the tower of a castle. The walls were of stone, ancient walls worn smooth. My bed covered half the room, a large semicircular bed where I would sit for hours, reading, reflecting, praying. There was a door, but it stayed shut. There was a window open to hills and trees, greenery. There was another little opening, through which my mother would give me food and drink and sometimes messages or letters. We would exchange a few words, a kiss, a smile, but that was all. It seemed natural to remain all alone in silence in my round room.

Now in reading Jung and in reflection, I see the importance of this dream. In giving it to me, my unconscious was answering a deep-seated longing. Our souls need the symbols of our dreams. Jung wrote volumes about the symbolic life and how it can express the needs of the soul. Even as a child, I needed my round bedroom, my towerlike dwelling, to where I could go alone, in quiet, undisturbed. Jung took this need concretely and built himself a tower, away from Kusnacht on the upper part of the Lake of Zurich at Bollingen. Over the years he built an annex, with a private meditation room, a place of spiritual concentration. He continued to build on it as he continued his journey into the psyche, into the soul. He painted family emblems of heraldry on the walls, he chiseled names and inscriptions on the stones. For Jung, the tower was the center of his life-long journey into the inner depths of the soul.

My round room comes back to me. It brings healing. As I sit now at my desk, writing about the cherry tree, writing about our youngest son, our other children, I go back into this round room and find rest. I close my eyes and enter it. I imagine myself alone, without interruptions, no one at the door, no one at the telephone. It is a timeless place, complete in itself. I read. I write. And I sit in quiet, not a dulling stillness which puts me to sleep, but a stillness which enlivens, which makes me more aware, which opens me to God's promptings, turning me inside out so that I see with the eyes of my soul.

My office, my writing space, becomes a tower. It reaches down to the cellar. Slowly I descend the steps into the dark-ness, leaving my desk, letting go of my books and journals. There, on the cellar walls of my imagination, I see the drag-ons that our youngest son painted when he was an adoles-cent. Dragons spitting fire, planes spewing bombs, cities in flame. The clouds of darkness thicken. I go still deeper and enter the chamber of the heart.

Here at the very ground of my being, I find again the prayer of the heart, the prayer of the desert fathers, invok-ing the name of Jesus Christ. "Lord Jesus Christ have mercy." The Eastern monks thought that by repeating untiringly the name of Jesus Christ, they would remain in the presence of God. God would come to inhabit their hearts. For years as a young mother, while my children were growing up, this was my prayer. Following the way of the Russian pilgrim—so well detailed in the anonymous narrative, *The Way of a Pilgrim*—I prayed the Jesus Prayer, this simple prayer of the desert fathers. I called and repeated the name of Jesus in order to enter into communion with each child, with my husband, with all of creation. "Lord Jesus Christ have mercy." "Lord have mercy." Sometimes the words slipped into Greek, "*Kýrie, eléison. Christe, eléison. Kýrie eléison,*" linking me back to the Eastern monks and joining all the many centuries of prayer in the repository of the church.

In this latter part of life, my prayer of the heart is most often without words. My tongue is stilled. My mind is stilled. The prayer of the heart becomes the heart's own respiration. I breathe in and I breathe out. It is God's breath. God breathing in, God breathing out. It is God's breath breathing me.

At the bottom of my tower, I touch water. The source bubbles and cascades, rushing out of the broken rock. It refreshes and cools my hands. The water ripples over my bare feet, rising above my ankles. I cup my hands to bring it up to my face. I drink its sweetness. It rises steadily. A strong wave surges. It washes clean the paintings of fiery dragons, of houses in flame, of burning skies, the paintings left on the walls. The wave continues to rise. I float on its curve, leaving the tower and the small round room of my dream. It carries me out to the front yard.

The cherry tree is in full blossom, each dark branch bursting with new life.

Legend of the Musk Deer

This legend was recounted by Hindu mothers to help their children understand that God is not outside their own beings but inside their own hearts.

Once upon a time, a very long time ago, the musk deer of the mountains was haunted by the scent of musked perfume. He bounded forth, from jungle to jungle in pursuit of the perfume. The poor animal gave up eating, drinking. He gave up even sleeping.

The musk deer did not know from where came the scent, nor did he know from where came his longing. But he was impelled to pursue it across ravines, forests and hills, until finally—starving, tormented, exhausted and straying aimlessly—he slipped from the summit of a boulder and fell mortally wounded.

His last act before he died was to take pity on himself and lick his chest which had ripped open in the fall on the rock. And there his musk pouch was pouring out its perfume.

The musk deer breathed in deeply, trying to inhale the perfume, but it was too late.[14]

Chapter Three:
Pear Tree

*Into this Dark, beyond all light, we pray to come and,
unseeing and unknowing, to see and to know Him that
is beyond seeing and beyond knowing....That is to do as
sculptors do, drawing the statue latent there...and dis-
playing the beauty hidden there.*

> Denis the Areopagite (Pseudo-Dionysius)

*For there is no light except that which proceeds from
darkness....And there is no worship of the Holy One
except that which comes from darkness....*

> Sefer Ha-Zohar, or Book of Splendor

*Seek Him in faith and love...by a way that thou knowest
not, to the hidden place of God. Because faith is like the
feet wherewith the soul journeys to God and love is the
guide that directs it.*

> St. John of the Cross, Spiritual Canticle

*The beauty of the world is the co-operation of divine wis-
dom in creation....All love of universal beauty proceeds
from God dwelling in our souls and goes out to God present in the universe.*

> Simone Weil, Waiting for God

The day I received the Van Gogh postcard...I saw the same pear tree in my front yard. The resemblance was uncanny.

Pear Tree
(Prose Poem)

Outside my window, in the middle of our front yard, leans a small pear tree. The trunk is dark gray. It puts out blossoms, skimpy ones on skinny branches. I wanted it out of sight. Planted many years ago, it grew crooked even with its wooden stake. When I finally pulled away the stake, I feared for its anorexic branches.

My husband's mother stood straight and strong in her large family. We were close to one hundred descendants on her eightieth birthday. She wore lavender, a soft full skirt, circling to the music of a waltz. Today, stricken with Alzheimer's disease, she sits strapped to a wheelchair, a woolen scarf tight across her chest. Her face is dazed in disbelief. Her eyes are dark gray circles. I look for light in them and find darkness. Her fingers try to fasten the last button on her sweater.

Today, a postcard of Van Gogh's painting Pear Tree in Bloom arrived. Its dark gray trunk is twisted, the branches ugly and crippled. But in the gnarled fists, there are bunches of color, mandalas of white blossoms, surrounded with a few dark green leaves.

started writing about the pear tree the day I received the Van Gogh postcard from a friend in Holland. Looking out my window, I saw the same pear tree in my front yard. The resemblance was uncanny. The tree outside my window was the same size, leaning the same way, with almost the identical number of crooked branches. Only the white blossoms looked different. The ones on my tree were sparse and sick looking. The ones on the postcard were full and glorious. But with time, one day, two days, one week, as I continued to gaze at them, my blossoms started to resemble the blossoms on Van Gogh's tree. The difference was in the person looking at them. Where I saw skimpy blossoms on crippled lifeless branches, Van Gogh saw abundant bunches of color.

My mind skipped to my mother-in-law, strapped into her wheelchair. Here too was a crippled figure. I had recently visited with her in the residence for older people in northern France, where she has lived since stricken with Alzheimer's. In the dark circles of her eyes, which looked so empty, could I now see blossoms of light? My prose poem shifted levels, from the pear tree to my mother-in-law and back to the pear tree. With bunches of color in gnarled fists.

The pear tree still grows crooked in the middle of our front yard. Its branches still are dark gray and twisted. And my mother-in-law still sits in her wheelchair. Very often, memories of my mother-in-law enter my mind and capture my imagination. In a very deep, unexpected way she has been involved in my destiny since our first meeting when I was a student at Grenoble University. It was a meeting that opened the door for my becoming Catholic. Another student and I were driving a friend to his home where a few hours earlier his younger sister had died after a long illness. Pierre was the oldest son of ten children. His sister Christine was twenty-one years old, my age.

A violent snowstorm delayed our arrival. Our car skidded off the road, we were stranded and would have to stay overnight at Pierre's home. It was midnight when his mother, in the midst of her grief, welcomed us at the door of their house. She asked if we wished to see Christine. Fear gripped me. I had never seen a dead person. I was in a foreign country, in a family I did not know. His mother sensed my anguish and showed me a spare room where I could rest and spend the night. My narrow bed was under the staircase leading to Christine's room. All night long, footsteps went up and down. The family was keeping vigil over Christine's body. As the storm surged against the window panes, footsteps echoed in the stairwell above my head. Heavy steps, lighter steps. I lay there without moving, petrified. Why hadn't I gone with Pierre and his friend when they continued up the staircase to see Christine? Why had I stayed behind, unable to speak one word?

All night the footsteps continued, there over my head. Fear flooded up from my childhood, filling the small spare room, submerging me. Where was my faith? I was in the shadow of the valley of death, but where was my shepherd's rod? His staff? They had stayed with me when I was small. Where were they now? I shivered with cold, wrestling with my fear as Jacob had wrestled with his angel. "Jacob was left alone. And there was one that wrestled with him until daybreak, who seeing that he could not master him, struck him in the socket of his hip...." (Genesis 32:25-26). Jacob did not let go until the angel blessed him. And so I wrestled with my angel, neither one of us giving up, until light filled my room. Until it was morning and I was washed over with tears.

Outside my window the storm had passed. There was silence. Silence as thick as the blanket of snow that fell during that night. I sat up on my bed and entered the stillness. I had no more questions. I had no answers either. But I was filled with grace. With an inward silence, blessed by my angel after wrestling in the dark. The faith of this family, resonating with the steps in the stairwell, had quieted my fear and taken me by the hand.

That summer when Pierre told his parents he was in love with the American student whom they had housed the night Christine died, his mother found it in her heart to welcome me again. She said the night the Lord took Christine, he brought Susan to their home. With these words she opened her arms to me, to her first future daughter-in-law. Her words were quite extraordinary. I was a stranger, an American, coming into a very French family. And I was Protestant, coming into a very traditional Catholic family.

Destiny? The word is not really mysterious. It is in reality a simple word, asking only that we live each present moment as it comes. It means being whom we are meant to be. As Meister Eckhart, the German Dominican, often said seven centuries earlier, a seed of a pear tree grows into a pear tree. Growing as we are intended to grow. Becoming whom we are meant to be. Accepting one's own reality. It means letting myself be blessed, letting myself be led by the hand. It means letting myself hear the words that Pierre's mother pronounced. She found the way to accepting me in her heart. She lived it as "willed," as destiny. In so doing, she unknowingly blessed me.

The next summer when I returned to France, I stayed at Pierre's house while he had a month of military training at Grenoble. During these weeks I often went to speak with the Dominican priest, Father Kaelin, who was to become so important in my life. I was taking instruction to learn more about the Catholic Church. I did not want to do this at home in Briarcliff. The village was small and our family was well known in the local Congregational church. It was Pierre's mother who suggested that I talk with the young Dominican who had assisted Christine during the last weeks before she died. He lived in a convent close by and found time to answer my questions with faith and love.

It was also Pierre's mother who gave me an invaluable book, Raissa Maritain's *Les Grandes Amitiés* (deep friendships). It is the story of Raissa's life, her early years in Russia, her school years in France, her studies of philosophy with her friend Jacques under the direction of Henri Bergson, their marriage and friendships with Leon Bloy, Charles Peguy, Jean Cocteau—names I had read at university, now illuminated by Raissa's friendship. And finally her discovery of a personal and transcendent God, leading to her conversion and baptism.

The book resonated deep in my heart. One morning when I was reading it—this memory is very clear—I said to myself, I too can embrace the Catholic faith. It was decided. There were no longer any questions, any hesitations. I asked Father Kaelin if he would welcome me into the Catholic Church that same summer. I chose the date of August 15, the feast of the Assumption of Mary, the Mother of God, wanting to open my heart to Mary, who was hidden away in my Protestant background. It rained lightly that August 15, but it was a beautiful day, with graces touching us like the drops of rain. All of Pierre's family were present, quietly standing around me. I wrote a letter to Raissa expressing my gratitude and asking for her prayers. She very quickly replied and we continued to correspond. She invited Pierre and me to come to their home near Princeton, New Jersey, where Jacques was teaching. It was there that she greeted us in 1958, a few months before our marriage.

Raissa was a contemplative. The depths of her soul shone forth in both her expression and her writing. She saw contemplation as overflowing into song and communion. In her journals, published by Jacques after her death, she wrote, "The intention of the river is to lose itself in the ocean, but if the riverbed is too full, it overflows to the left and to the right. The intention of the contemplative soul is to lose itself in God, but if the heart is too full, it overflows in poetic song and in acts."[15] She lived daily the tension of being a contemplative in a world of action and intellect. She saw her place next to her husband, Jacques, opening their home to all those who came to their door. "It would be an error to isolate oneself from mankind...if God does not call to solitude, it is necessary to live with God in the multitude and there to help make him known and loved."[16]

Raissa wrote also of darkness and difficulty and suffering, "We walk in darkness, stumbling upon a thousand obstacles. But we know that 'God is Love,' and our confidence in God is our light."[17] Today these words speak to me still more strongly than they did forty years ago. This was the woman my future mother-in-law introduced me to when she gave me her book. This was the woman who with such grace and unassuming kindness extended her greeting to me as she did to all those who were fortunate to meet her.

When now I look in Maman's eyes, I look for bunches of white flowers. When I go for the weekend in the residence where she remains alone since Papa died, I spend long moments with her. When I speak with her and she hears my American accent, she looks at me deeply. Behind the veil of forgetfulness, I believe she remembers. Remembers the first night I arrived in her home, the night when Christine died. Remembers the old stone church at Samoëns where I knelt for the first time at the altar to receive the Eucharist. Step by step, from my keeping company with God as a child to my hours of prayer as an adolescent, I had been led to this sacrament, to the mystery of God's incarnation in Christ, and through Christ in each one of us, the mystery of the continuing incarnation.

I take Maman to the chapel at the residence and together we pray. We are alone. I push her wheelchair down the middle aisle, in front of the altar where today there are freshly gathered lilies of the valley. Their fragrance overflows. I bring the bouquet of tiny flowers close for her to smell. They smell so sweet, she wants to taste them. She opens her lips. I put the bouquet back on the altar. She closes her eyes. Is she farther away than when her eyes are open? Can I enter into this unknowing? Can I leave behind me my willful desire to understand—to discover how much she is present—and dwell in this place of un-seeing? Can I close my eyes and sit in front of God's altar?

I look for passages in *The Cloud of Unknowing*, the beautiful book written by an unnamed medieval monk, most likely a Cistercian or Carthusian priest of the fourteenth century, addressing a young disciple about the practice of contemplative prayer. The author advises him that such prayer takes place only in darkness, in a privation of knowing.

> This darkness and cloud is always between you and
> your God, no matter what you do....So set yourself to
> rest in this darkness as long as you can, always cry-
> ing out after him whom you love. For if you are to
> experience him, insofar as it is possible here, it must
> always be in this cloud and in this darkness.
>
> *The Cloud of Unknowing*[18]

To rest in this darkness as long as possible. I am to rest in this opaque unknowing, leaving behind the light of understanding. To no longer want to understand, to no longer need to understand, only to cry out to God whom I love.

As I rest in this cloud of darkness between me and my God, so am I to rest in still another cloud between me and the others. "Just as this cloud of unknowing is above you between you and your God, in the same way you must put beneath you a cloud of forgetting between you and all the creatures that have ever been made."[19] As long as I am full of myself and of other creatures, I cannot rest still in such a cloud. Only in forgetting everything can the disciple reach out to God. When I forget something, it is wrapped in darkness. Then it is as though my mind has been emptied. However when I remember something, my mind is filled with this memory, encumbered with the distraction of remembering. Whatever comes into my mind comes between me and my God. If God is to be all in all—"so that God may be all in all" (1 Cor15:28)—there is no room for us to be something else. When all is forgotten, when there is nothing but darkness, then am I able to reach out freely, without attachment, toward God.

I sit in the chapel next to my mother-in-law. Only recently do I willingly rest in this darkness. When we were together during the early years of her Alzheimer's disease, we used to recite the Our Father or a Hail Mary. I would listen and steal glances at her to reassure myself that she was saying the prayer with me. I wanted her to repeat the words. Then when she stopped moving her lips, I still continued to say the words aloud. Now as she sits unmoving, I no longer pray aloud with words in her presence. I close my eyes and move into darkness. I do not know where she is. I forget for a moment where I am. A space of unknowing. A cloud of unknowing. There is nothing. Nothing. Our medieval author would correct me. He would say that only the outward man calls it nothing. "Who is he that calls it nothing? It is surely our outward man, not our inward. Our inward man calls it All."[20] It is the All that welcomes me when I close my eyes and sit still, when I leave behind my outward self, making room for my inner self and letting it take over on its own.

It is this inward self who sees the beauty of the crooked pear tree. It flapped its anorexic wings and instead of falling over, it grew bunches of flowers in its gnarled fists. What was it that made me see the tree as anorexic? Were those white blossoms so skimpy that they hurt? The word *anorexic* was not chosen by accident. In the pear tree I saw also an image of our anorexic daughter trying to survive. It was when she was far from home at university, that she started to stop eating. There was no wooden stake, stuck in the ground to hold her straight. She lost twelve kilos. I remember when she telephoned from the pay phone. The phone dropped from her hand. I heard it rattle against the metal door. She did not pick it up. I called her name. The receiver went dead. I shouted. No answer. No one. The lifeline, daughter-mother, was cut.

I prayed. I prayed tears. How can a mother let her daughter starve herself? When she came home and I took her in my arms, I thought she would break in my embrace. She felt brittle like the branches of the pear tree. I cried and I prayed. I prayed to know what to do. I carried her in my heart. By nature we carry all our children in our hearts. But sometimes we carry especially close to us one or the other of our children. Prayer becomes like a strong hug. We center ourselves in God's love, and then we summon into the circle our loved ones.

There is the idea of the mandala here. As we breathe in God's love, our prayer gathers inward. We gather strength. Then as we breathe out, our prayer reaches outward. Our family, our friends, all our intentions, are gathered into the circle. Then we release them, as we breathe out God's love over them, around them. This happens naturally. We do not need to think about it. We are like prayer wheels. In this way I prayed for my daughter.

For three years she counted the calories of crackers and cheese, of half a hard-boiled egg, of carrot salad with lemon juice. She sliced the apple into twelve portions for the twelve hours of the day. Straight A's were not enough. There had to be highest honors. She smiled and shook the dean's hand. It was a game of roulette. Life or death. It would be so easy, she said. Like her first boyfriend, who crashed into a tree. But she chose to live. She picked herself up and worked her way up the ladder of professional success to the top. Like a trapeze artist, she was swinging way up high.

And on her wedding day, she chose again. She was in love. She would marry and hopefully have a family. She carried white flowers as fragile as herself. She stood at the open door of the ancient church of Samoëns, where centuries of prayer hold the stones together in the thick walls and where thirty years earlier I had embraced the Catholic faith. I knew the path to the doorway by heart.

At the open door of the ancient church of Samoëns
where centuries of prayer hold the stones together....

I close my eyes and see the white flowers. Her fragile silhouette disappears in the cloud of forgetting. I enter the darkness. This is how the author instructed the young disciple. As the cloud of unknowing lies between us and our God, so the cloud of forgetting lies between us and all creatures. All creatures and all thoughts of creatures. "And whenever I say 'all the creatures that have ever been made,' I mean not only the creatures themselves, but also all their works and circumstances. I make no exceptions, whether they are bodily creatures or spiritual....In short, I say that all should be hidden under the cloud of forgetting."[21]

As I cry out after God, I let the image of my daughter in her white dress at the doorway of the church hide itself in the darkness. I no longer consciously summon her into my space of prayer. I sit instead in this cloud of forgetting without images, without words, with only the longing for God. Waiting in silence. "For God alone my soul waits in silence; for my hope is from him" (Psalm 62).

Here too should be hidden even our thoughts of God, for God cannot be thought. My finite mind is incapable of grasping the infinite mind of God. If I persist and try to conceptualize God, the "Being" that I carefully conceive will resemble my mind, not God's. Likewise if I try to imagine God, again the "Being" that I carefully imagine will resemble my imagination and not God's. Only God can think of God. Only God can imagine God. But God can be loved. In darkness, I can love God. I can close my eyes. My thoughts grow dim, my mind slows down. There is an emptying. The thinking "I," the controlling "I," the ego, disappears. Only then is there room for God's love to take hold of us.

The cloud of unknowing becomes the place where I encounter God. I close my eyes and enter this space of forgetting, this hiding place. I do not see God, but I enter into God's seeing. In this cloud, I become part of God's seeing. There is the sudden echo in the Pauline text, "It is no longer I who live but Christ who lives in me" (Galatians 2:20 RSV). Saint Paul here defines his life as communion with the Son of God. It is no longer the old Paul living on his own, but it is the new Paul living at one with Christ.

When I am so emptied, of images, of thoughts, even of loved ones, the old me disappears. I am no longer the person I used to know, the person I thought I knew. Saint Paul talked of getting rid of the old self. "You must put aside your old self...so that you can put on the new self that has been created in God's way" (Ephesians 4:22-24). The unknown author of *The Cloud of Unknowing* wrote about the outer man and the inner man. Once I have gotten rid of the outer man, the old self, then the inner man, the new self reborn in Christ, is the one who acts. This is powerful imagery, to be reborn in Christ. Christ is the transformative medium. The new self is created in the image of God. I nourish this transformation through the Eucharist. Each time that the bread and wine are consecrated, that they become the presence of Christ, so too is the creation consecrated, so too am I consecrated. So too do I become a sacrament—visible sign of invisible grace—of Christ's presence as he acts through me.

But at this moment, I am sitting in darkness. I am praying. I am pushing away all thoughts. It is the time of forgetting, the time of unknowing. Afterward, when I arise from prayer, I will see—with God's grace—a different dimension in everything. I will see with God's eyes. When I look at the blossoms on the pear tree, I will see their abundant whiteness. The colors will be deeper, the green leaves will refresh me. When I look into my mother-in-law's eyes, I will see her understanding.

When I look at my daughter, I will see her strength. When I look around me, I will see God's presence in my surroundings. I will touch a deeper level. I will live from a deeper level.

God's level. A level from which I was separated when I was born, when I acquired an outer nature that does not always accord itself to my inner nature. Reaching to touch God's level is not a blind returning to the Garden of Eden, but rather a conscious return. From this level, I will see God's world as God sees it. I will look out my window and see the front yard ablaze in God's love. The forsythia bush will glow and catch fire in the sunlight. I will look down the street and see my neighbors clothed in God's goodness, both the neighbors I know and those I do not know. Their faces will shine, their arms will open. Compassion will fill my heart. Love will overflow. There will be communion.

Let me return to Thomas Merton, for this "seeing" is the epiphany that he described so beautifully in his journal, when suddenly on the corner of the street in Louisville, he looked at mankind and loved them.

> In Louisville, at the corner of Fourth and Walnut, in the center of the shopping district, I was suddenly overwhelmed with the realization that I loved all those people, that they were mine and I theirs, that we could not be alien to one another even though we were total strangers. It was like waking from a dream of separateness, of spurious self-isolation in a special world, the world of renunciation and supposed holiness. The whole illusion of a separate holy existence is a dream.
>
> *Conjectures of a Guilty Bystander*[22]

Such an epiphany of God's presence overwhelms. God lets us see the world with different eyes. Merton felt suddenly alive to the world. He had been living in a "dream of separateness." The oneness of all humanity becomes a reality. So also the oneness and beauty of all creation. I think of my pear tree and its skimpy flowers. The love of God flowers in its branches. The anorexic tree becomes green and full of new life. The white blossoms are immense.

Again I am skipping ahead. I am not out on the streets of Fourth and Walnut in Louisville. I am not experiencing an epiphany. Instead I am dwelling in darkness and groping for words to explain no words. I am looking for how to write about no words. I search, and I lose my way in this dark hovering.

Once my willful thinking is gone and once my personal desire is gone, once I have lost my way, then what is left of me is utterly free to reach out to God. It is as if I have shed everything that is myself, leaving only a "no-self." The fifth-century theologian Proclus teaches that there is in us, underneath our awareness, underneath all our powers of mind and imagination, a "no thing." Something that is utterly unidentifiable, that is therefore a no thing. It is this no thing that is drawn to the No Thing which is God. I linger in this paradox. A paradox where at last my mind gives up. God is No Thing. Yet God is All. *Deus est.* God is not the object. God is the subject. In my no-thing-ness, I become part of the No-Thing-ness of God. I become part of the All which is God.

When precisely I lose consciousness of myself and I see my no-thing-ness, when my senses are numbed and my limbs paralyzed, when I want to give up and return to "normality," it is then that the medieval teacher, author of *The Cloud*, tells me to press on.

> Carry on then with that nothing, as long as you are
> doing it for God's love. Do not leave off, but press on

earnestly in that nothing with an alert desire in your
will to have God, whom no man can know. For I tell
you truly I would rather be in this way nowhere bodily, wrestling with this blind nothing, than to have
such power that I could be everywhere bodily.

The Cloud of Unknowing[23]

Wrestling with this blind nothing, I sit next to my mother-
in-law in the chapel and push aside all conscious thoughts
of her, all conjectures, of wondering where she is. I push
aside all conscious thoughts of myself, of wondering
where I am. As the veil lowers itself over her gaze, so does
it lower itself over my gaze. There occurs a cleansing, an
emptying. I sink into the dense cloud and let her very forgetfulness teach me forgetfulness.

Wrestling with this blind nothing, I watch my anorexic
daughter walk on the borderline, struggling to keep her balance. I close my eyes and see her strength. She picks herself
up and finds her way. I still my voice. I think of Demeter wel-
coming her daughter Persephone each springtime, knowing
that in autumn she will leave again and return to the
Underworld. I see my daughter standing at the threshold. I
let her show me the darkness.

This has become my way of prayer—in the words of our
unknown author, "a dark gazing into the simple being of
God alone."

The Sacred Hoop

This sacred vision of Black Elk, the Sioux holy man, lifts up the hearts of those who listen, offering a vision of oneness of all creation.

I looked ahead and saw the mountains there with rocks and forests on them, and from the mountains flashed all colors upward to the heavens.

Then I was standing on the highest mountain of them all, and round about beneath me was the whole hoop of the world.

And while I stood there I saw more than I can tell, and I understood more than I saw; for I was seeing in a sacred manner the shapes of all things in the spirit, and the shape of all shapes as they must live together like one being.

And I saw that the sacred hoop of my people was one of many hoops that made one circle, wide as daylight and as starlight, and in the center grew one mighty flowering tree to shelter all the children of one mother and one father.

And I saw that it was holy.[24]

CHAPTER FOUR:
ACORN

*Make your home in me, as I make mine in you....I am
the vine, you are the branches. Whoever remains in me,
with me in him, bears fruit in plenty.*

John 15:4-5

*From the gentle layer of air, moisture effervesces over
the earth. This wakens the earth's greenness and causes
all fruits to put forth seeds and become fertile.*

Hildegard of Bingen, Scivias

*God gives his Son birth in the most inward part of the
spirit, and that is the inner world. Here God's ground is
my ground, and my ground is God's ground.*

Meister Eckhart, Essential Sermons

*To let each impression and each germ of a feeling come
to completion wholly in itself, in the dark, in the inex-
pressible, the unconscious, beyond the reach of one's
own intelligence and await with humility and patience
the birth-hour of a new clarity.*

Rainer Maria Rilke, Letters to a Young Poet

*It is a very small acorn, so small
that it has slipped out of its loose husk.*

Acorn
(Prose Poem)

I found an acorn rolled far from its mother oak tree. It is a very small acorn, so small that it has slipped out of its loose husk. The shell is smooth and golden brown, reflecting the light of the morning sun. The husk is perfectly woven, like a Native American basket. The tiny point at the end of the round shell is searching for something. At its base a dark lotus-like mandala is engraved.

My mother, aged eighty-eight, has slipped out of the deep depression that has been with her much of her life. Her skin is still smooth. I remember washing her back in the shower at the seaside. Its soft nudity made me think of an oil painting of a lovely young bather, a painting that used to hang in my parents' bedroom. In growing old, my mother has shed her depression. She moves lightly, following the path imprinted in her soul.

I have read that the tree inside a seed is extremely small but that it has all its essential parts. There is a tiny white thread that will one day turn into the trunk. The thread has a root tip at one end and a bud at the other. When the seed is ripe, it opens. The end with the root will point downward, deep into the earth. I have read that if it opens the other way, the seed will turn itself around.

My mother has the habit of daily prayer. Even in periods of depression, she reads her morning prayers and her evening prayers. When we visit together, each morning, before breakfast, she calls me to listen to her morning meditations. She subscribes to her church's *Daily Word* magazine. And for the last fifty years she has been reading over and over each month the same meditation book, hardbound and faded gray, two pages for each day. There is a text on the right-hand side and an open page on the left where she notes with a minimum of words important happenings, "Hollie [her husband, my father] is in the hospital," "Had Thanksgiving with my two daughters," "Alleluia, a new grandson," and on another page, "Alleluia again, a new great grandson."

She reads in order first the Bible reading in the *Daily Word*, followed by the long text of meditation in the gray book, and then she gives me her comments. She'll want me to say that the words speak to me the same way they speak to her. Sometimes I cannot say this yet I do not want to disappoint her. I try to find a loving way to phrase my thoughts. The mother-daughter bond holds me in its grip.

Likewise, before she goes to bed, she calls me to her room to listen to her evening meditations. Quite recently, while listening—the readings are rather long—my mind skipped back to the words of the evening prayer she taught me to say every night in bed: "Now I lay me down to sleep, I pray the Lord my soul to keep. And if I die before I wake, I pray the Lord my soul to take." The words surfaced with a jolt. In a way they are frightening. They are not part of the prayer scene that I summon up when I think about my childhood. Maybe I never thought about their meaning. Praying the Lord my soul to take. They were more part of the ritual of going to bed, of pulling the covers up and receiving a good-night kiss. Now it is I who pull the covers up for my mother and give her a good-night kiss. The bond has become daughter-mother.

When I was collecting acorns and writing about them, my mother was coming out of two years of intense depression. If a depression can be compared to the husk of an acorn, she has carried the husk most of her life. By moments its relentless weight was intolerable. Now she has shed it. When I went to see her, she looked smaller, as though condensed, living each day gratefully, freely, happily. No longer was she waking in the morning wishing she had not awakened, wishing rather she had stayed forever asleep. She lives in Williamsburg near my only sister, who watches over her. This September she came to visit us in Europe. She saw her grandchildren and all her great-grandchildren—the ones on this side of the ocean—including the youngest, the tenth. When she was leaving, sitting in the section of the airport for people needing assistance, waiting to be wheeled into the plane, she turned to me and said, "Thank heavens, I lived until today."

Thankful to have lived until today. What a beautiful gift she gave me with those words. A gift of love and faith. Meister Eckhart said that if the only prayer we say in our whole life is "thank you," that would suffice. We thank God for life. We thank God by becoming what we are. The acorn thanks God by becoming an oak tree. It cracks its shell and goes deep into the ground. So it is for my mother. She thanks God in growing from an only child to the mother, grandmother, and great-grandmother, flying over the ocean at eighty-eight years old. Her roots reach deep. Her depressions were the husk weighing her down. They were also the crack, opening her to the light in the darkness. She's all right with the night, she's all right with the day. What's ahead, none of us can spell out. But she is ready. And I think that if she were again turned upside down, she'd struggle once more to turn herself around.

The crack opens us to the potential hidden deep within us. According to Aristotle, an acorn grows into an oak tree because it has the form of the oak tree within its soul. It was Descartes's thinking, in the seventeenth century, that took the souls away from the trees and the animals and situated them somewhere in the human brain. Before Descartes, all of creation was seen as a living being with a soul. The Platonists spoke of the *anima mundi*, the soul of the world. As a child I hugged trees. Conversing with God, I hugged my rock. It felt warm and alive. As did the round trunk of the tree. Then I was warned that this was pantheism. The tree was not God. God was not the tree. So I stopped talking to trees in order to grow up, to be adult. Until I decided it was all right to be a pantheist or a pan-entheist to be more precise. God is not the tree, but God is in the tree. Or still better, the tree is in God.

Now again we are seeing that the soul is not something that only we humans are blessed to carry around with us, up in our brain, but that it is the animating force of the entire universe. In the new sciences, soul is reintroduced in the concept of the field. Nature is constantly being reanimated through invisible fields. So soul is likened to a field in the heart of matter, giving form to creation and holding it all together. Fields are unlimited in time and space. They are the world we live in. This is very different from the mechanistic thinking we grew up with, the thinking that says the soul is up in our head somewhere. Instead, as Hildegard of Bingen—the incredible teacher, healer, composer, mystic of the twelfth century—explained, the soul is not in the body, but rather the body is in the soul.

The body is in this immeasurable unending field. *Field* is a wonderful word. A field stretches out, a field goes deep, a field is to grow in, to play in. I remember the fields that surrounded the white farmhouse where I lived until I was five years old. They reached out in all directions with wooden fences as spokes. Out to a circumference that was always widening. The concept of *field* brings back the parable in the Gospel of Matthew that Jesus told about the man sowing a mustard seed in his field.

> The kingdom of heaven is like a mustard seed which a man took and sowed in his field. It is the smallest of all the seeds, but when it has grown it is the biggest shrub of all and becomes a tree so that the birds of the air come and shelter in its branches.
>
> Matthew 13:31–32

A small seed sowed in the field. I am back to the part of darkness in my prayer. As the seed opens in the ground, so the soul opens in the ground, in the dark. Over the last decade, with each faltering step I took into this darkness, my prayer—a prayer of no words—found deeper roots. This way of prayer is called apophatic, the dark way of silence. This way takes leave of discourse, of the mind, and turns to the heart, the dwelling place of God. This is the prayer of the early desert fathers, the Orthodox prayer of the heart, the prayer of Saint Teresa, of Saint John of the Cross, of the *Cloud of Unknowing,* of Meister Eckhart, of

Thomas Merton and of countless others. The other way of prayer is called kataphatic, the way of light, the way that talks about God, that defines God's being, that affirms God's perfection. The oak tree in full foliage praises the Creator, but in order to become the oak tree in full foliage, the acorn has to open in the dark. Its roots have to reach deep into the earth as its branches stretch toward the light.

There in the dark the shell has to crack. As I enter this dwelling place of God, as I fall into the very ground of my being, burying myself in the darkness, I have to open. I have to find the crack that lights even the darkest of nights. This is "the dark light" of Saint John of the Cross. If I have no cracks, I become sufficient onto myself. Sufficient even in the dark, luring myself into thinking that I am comfortable there in the dark, that this is it, that this is the dark night of the soul. Not so. This is all me. This is my thought, my darkness, my night. Only when I let go of my protective shell, when I find the crack that makes me vulnerable, that opens me to the Other, only then will the night be radiant, only then will the dark be light.

I grasped this reality with my mind long before I lived it in my heart. I even wrote about it in one of my first stories, "The Water Jug," a true story, the meaning of which I am still discovering. Many years ago, when the children were quite young, I was driving home from a day of silence spent at the monastery with the Sisters of Bethlehem, up on top of the Voirons, northeast of Geneva and across the border in France. This is where I still go for moments of quiet and prayer. The little sisters make earthenware pottery for a livelihood, and this particular visit I chose a water jug where the rings of clay were visible. One of the sisters wrapped it in a sheet of newspaper and walked me to the gate to say good-bye.

I was alone in the car. It was summer time. I stopped to pick a few wild flowers. Continuing down the narrow winding road, I heard a bee in the back of the car. It circled around my head and lunged through the steering wheel. I looked up and saw a stone cliff straight in front of me. The car did a somersault, lifting itself up in slow motion before I fainted. Pulling myself out of the wreckage, I picked up my water jug in the middle of the road and lay down on the side of the mountain. An ambulance took me the rest of the way, down to the hospital in Geneva. I was not hurt. X-rays showed nothing broken. Pierre came to drive me home. I was still holding the water jug. I undid the newspaper. It was whole, intact, not a scratch. But over the months and years, a fine line started to etch itself onto the ringed surface of the jug, like a vein, slowly becoming visible, slowly climbing upward. The crack was inside the water jug, making the jug vulnerable.

The same crack is inside us. We are by our very nature vulnerable. There is a fault line, separating us from our Creator. But we have to find the crack. Even when I wrote this story, that the jug had to roll over with the car and still wait for years before showing its crack, I did not understand its meaning. I had lived through this accident, I had written a story about it. And still I did not see my own crack. No X-ray showed it.

It reminds me of a story that our priest here in Geneva told a few years later. There is a mountain climber who is struggling to reach the top of the summit; he's almost there when he slips and falls over the side. He grips on to the branch of a single sapling that grows out of the rocky cliff and hangs there above the precipice. He looks up and calls, "Is anyone up there?" At first no one answers. He

The crack was inside the water jug....
The same crack is inside us.

calls again. "Is anyone there?" A voice answers, "Yes, I am here." "Who are you?" the man asks. "I am God. Let go." There is silence. Then the mountain climber calls out again, "Is there anyone else?"

I was not ready to let go. I had to literally break myself, to crack my body, in order to finally learn to let go. So it happened. I was rushing down the wooden staircase in our house when I lost my footing and started tumbling down the steps on my back. I reached out with my right arm and caught part of the banister. Something snapped. It was my shoulder. I went from doctor to doctor. Surgery was the only possible solution but the shoulder would be forever stiff. Instead I changed my way of living. No more heavy housework. No more active sports. An electronic typewriter, eventually a computer. I could not even write by hand.

I went within. Hours opened up to me. Nights opened up. Very often I was awake with pain, I could not sleep. And days opened up. There was less I could do. I learned to sit still. This was in the mid-1980s. The time of my father's death. The time of my first reading of Jung. The time of my reawakening to a vibrant faith in God and to a deep sense of communion with all of creation. It was when I started hugging trees again. Unexpectedly I was given time to pray and to write. Writing became a way of prayer. I'd sit with my eyes closed, letting my fingers move over the keyboard as I listened to my heart speak.

The other way of prayer was without words. I was taking my first steps into silent prayer, just sitting in God's presence or in God's absence, as it often seemed. I longed for his presence and so I sat in silence, waiting. And a few years later, when darkness seeped into my family life, with bouts of violence, anger, jealousy, depression, drugs and anorexia, with a husband very often far away in another world, in his world of business, I had a shield ready.

A shield of silent prayer. I knew I could not cope alone. My achieving ego, my controlling mind, were unequal to the task. I could not alone make things right. For years I had thought I could. Everything would be all right. The children still tell me that I was forever saying, "It's all right." But it was no longer all right. And it was out of my hands. It was in God's hands. I was in God's hands. Struggling to ward off the demons of disunity and despair. I was holding up my shield. For me, for my youngest son, for my daughter, for the other children, each with their own bruises and burdens. A shield of power and protection. Holding it up again and again. With tears. Higher. Centering myself. Centering our family. And love came through. Came through the cracks and held us together.

My cracked shoulder was given to me as the metaphor of my opening to the dark. I wanted to go down still deeper, no longer only intellectually through books, but physically through my entire being. To live on a deeper level. To write on a deeper level. To pray on a deeper level. To let myself fall into the dark. Down into my roots, into Jung's universal unconscious, that immense timeless pool of human experience, into that great underground river which Eckhart imaged as God. It was this incredibly deep longing for darkness that took me into Jungian analysis.

During the first long dark winter of analysis, I was led by the hand to the Black Madonna. I traveled to Einsiedeln to see a friend at a Jungian conference. Upon arrival she took me to see the legendary statue of the Black Madonna, which I have since written about in *Looking for Gold*. The original statue belonged to Saint Meinrad, who went to live as a hermit way back in 822 A.D. in the Finsterwald, the dark forest, south of Zurich in the mountains. There he built a small sanctuary for the statue, dedicating it to the Mother of God. Upon this site stands the Benedictine Abbey of Einsiedeln. Meinrad's statue is preserved in a small sanctuary within the very large baroque church. Over the centuries the statue darkened, and the legend of the Black Madonna grew, bringing more and more pilgrims to her side, pilgrims looking for healing, drawn to this darker side of Mary, the Mother of God, the side that welcomes our darkness.

I had never felt close to Mary. As an adult, when welcomed into the Catholic Church, I intentionally chose to add the name of Mary to my name, Susan. I had rendered her the traditional prayers, reciting the rosary, honoring her alongside her Son, but I had never been deeply attached to her veneration. The cherubic white and blue statues of Virgin Mary remained lifeless in the corners of my faith as in the corners of the churches that I visited.

Now in Einsiedeln, when I entered the immense baroque church of the ancient Benedictine Abbey, I felt first a wave of nausea. Everything was so ornate, I felt I was inside a giant coral-colored wedding cake. But at one end of the immense nave, I saw the small chapel of the Black Madonna. I walked and stood in front of the sanctuary. Inside, all was gold—the small altar, the candelabras, the tabernacle, and above it the statue of the Madonna, crowned in gold and dressed in a gilded sumptuous robe, the Christ Child also crowned and dressed in brocade, against a backdrop of gold. But underneath the trappings, the Madonna and the Child were black.

I knelt down and closed my eyes to everything but the blackness. I entered it. Nothing else mattered. Everything else disappeared. It was the black hole of my childhood nightmares, but it went beyond the remembered tunnel with an extraordinary impression of both fullness and emptiness. I was without words, without thoughts. I simply was. Or rather the Black Madonna simply was. So fully had she welcomed me, I was no longer there.

Where did her blackness come from? The memory of older pagan statues of Artemis in Greece, of Isis in Egypt, of Ishtar in Sumeria? Of the Great Mother Goddess? Or the many fires that had destroyed the sanctuary? Or the smoke of thousands upon thousands of candles burning day and night in front of her? Or did the darkness come from her compassion, her motherhood, which suffers and permits suffering?

It was the latter, her overwhelming compassion, that brought me to my knees. Mary, the Mother of God, permits and blesses my darkness. She blesses my suffering. She blesses my brokenness, the pieces chipped away in leaving my home, my family, my country and language, in giving birth to new life, in tending to the tempers of each child. She waits for me there where I hurt. Where I have no words. She gathers the pieces together. My pieces but also the pieces of those dear to me. The pieces of my family. The broken pieces of my children. All the pieces gathered together in the dark, in the dark embrace of the Mother of God.

I came away from this visit feeling different. Again I am using words to try to describe something beyond words. But still in opening the door to the darkness of the Black Madonna, I opened the door to her compassion. A wave of love flowed through me. I return here to Saint Teresa's image, in the middle of her interior castle, the image of a huge wave, carrying the soul in its current. No longer was Mary the cherubic white and blue statue. She was the radiant black Mother of God. She was Mothergod. Her dark womb was the womb of enlightenment. She was Gaia, Mother Earth. The mother of all the creation. She was waiting for me in the darkness, where the seed opens to new life.

There was another Black Madonna waiting for me much closer to Geneva—the Black Madonna of Monts Voirons, near the monastery where I so often went to pray with the sisters, where I bought my water jug. On a more recent visit, one afternoon before vespers, I went for a walk in the woods on the side of the mountain overlooking the Lake of Geneva. I followed a narrow path, overrun with roots and stones, holding my thoughts—and myself—as still as possible. The path went deep into the dark trees before coming to a clearing, where there was an abandoned chapel. I pushed open the heavy door. In front of me, on a small wooden shelf in the stone wall behind the altar, stood a dark Madonna and Child. Illuminated by a shaft of sunlight from a window to the southwest, she was looking right at me, almost smiling, holding her infant child on her hip. I went closer and stood very still in front of her open regard.

She was not dressed in silk brocade. Her skin was not jet black, but the dark aged skin of a tree. There was no crown. Neither on her head nor on the infant Jesus. There was no gold. Only the late afternoon sunlight, shining on her face, casting a shadow behind her on the stone wall. There was no one else in the church. She was waiting there for me alone.

How many times had I driven up to the monastery, how many times had I spent an afternoon, a day, a weekend there on top of the mountain? But never had I adventured into the woods, never had I stumbled upon the path leading to the chapel. And all these years the Black Madonna of Monts Voirons was waiting. For centuries she waits, dark like the

The Black Madonna of Monts Voirons....
For centuries she waits, dark like the wood.

woods, regardless of time, waiting humbly in silence, the missing darkness of the feminine side of God, the all-embracing quality of the Mother.

I entered into her womb of darkness with my longings and my sorrows. I stood there, now a grandmother, carrying my family in my heart. I knew what the act of birth involved. I knew the dying to oneself that tears open the womb as the child is born. I had suffered this for each one of our children, feeling in my depths that this new life in my womb was too big for both it and me to survive. And then I knew the eruption of new life. The eruption no words can touch. An explosion. New life clamoring to be nurtured. Now it was Mary the Mother of God, waiting to give birth to the child of God within me. Within her womb, I connected anew with the core of my being. For an instant of eternity, I experienced oneness, with God and with all of creation.

A grandmother finding wholeness one afternoon in front of the Black Madonna on the side of the mountain. In front of a statue that dates back to the Middle Ages, to 1451, when a lord of the region, the Lord of Langins—mortally wounded by a wild boar—made a vow and was healed by the Virgin Mary. Fulfilling his vow, he built a chapel close to where he had fallen and placed a wooden statue of Our Lady on the small altar. Over the years the statue drew more and more pilgrims to her side. Already in the sixteenth century, she was described as being dark like a Moorish woman, linking her to the fiancée in the Song of Songs.

> I am dark but lovely,
> daughters of Jerusalem,
> like the tents of Kedar,
> like the pavilions of Salmah.

Take no notice of my swarthiness,
it is the sun that has burnt me.
Song of Songs, 1:5-6

Dark and lovely. This is how I find her each time I return to stand in silence at her feet. As I walk through the woods—a place of growth and life, but also of decay and death—my heart attunes itself to the all-embracing quality of the mother. The mother inside me knows that there must be decay for growth, there must be death for life. And as I open the door to the abandoned chapel, I feel engulfed in the Mother outside me. Her darkness welcomes my darkness, and the darkness of my children and grandchildren. It roots me, both physically and spiritually, down into the earth, back through the centuries to the Mother Goddess.

All the way back to Wisdom, to God's helpmate, who was there at his side before the world was created. She covered the earth like mist, she searched where to pitch her tent, she placed her roots in the Lord's property. "I was beside the master craftsman, delighting him day after day, ever at play in his presence, at play everywhere on his earth, delighting to be with the children of men" (Proverbs 8:30). With thoughts wider than the sky, she displays her strength from one end of the earth to the other, ordering all things for good. It was to Wisdom that Solomon prayed. "I entreated, and the spirit of Wisdom came to me. I esteemed her more than scepters and thrones; compared with her, I held riches as nothing" (Wisdom 7:7-8). More splendid than the sun, she is the untarnished reflection of God's goodness.

Wisdom greets me in the Black Madonna. She reveals to me my true nature. A nature that holds life and death together. A nature that admits pain, longing, suffering.

I come to her looking for healing, for wholeness. As she mends the broken parts, she reveals the pattern underneath the pieces. I understand better who I am. A child of God. And in so doing, I begin to see the true nature of those I carry in my heart, to understand better who they are. They too, with their brokenness, are children of God. They become uniquely lovable. My husband, my children, my grandchildren. His family on this side of the ocean. My family on the other side—my mother, my sister, her family. And my friends, the ones I see very often and the ones I see less.

Each of us has our unique destiny. Our stories are imprinted in our souls. Like the petal-shaped mandala engraved on the shell of the acorn, so my destiny is imprinted on the shell of my soul. In the dark the shell breaks and turns toward the light. The acorn grows to be an oak tree. In the dark I crack and open to the light. I grow to be the person that I am.

Soul is the field within, where I can pitch my tent and play in the presence of the Lord. Soul is also the field without, where all of creation bows down. Soul is both individual, there in my depths, and universal, going beyond, beyond all that I can imagine. My destiny, the thread hidden in the acorn seed, is uniquely mine. As is the destiny of each of our children. But destinies, like souls, overlap and embrace. I think of the extraordinary Native American image, "the net of gems," where in every gem of the net there is the reflection of all the other gems.

My silent prayer, the spoken and unspoken prayers of my husband and of my children, they join in the same chorus, the same outpouring of love. Our hands touch one another. Our souls reflect one another. The hands of all the creation clap in unison.

Acorn

Acclaim Yahweh, all the earth,
   burst into shouts of joy!...
Let the sea thunder and all that it holds,
   and the world, with all who live in it;
let all the rivers clap their hands
   and the mountains shout for joy.

Psalm 98 JB

Tale of the Young Lover

This Sufi parable invites the listener deep into transparency. It is the story of the lover whose heart has room only for the beloved.

A lover, arrogant and daring, goes out into the dark night to knock at the door of his beloved. She asks, "Who is there?" Proudly, he answers, "It is I." She refuses to open the door and tells him to go away.

The young man, full of anger, goes away declaring that he will forget her, that indeed he has already forgotten her. He travels around the immense world. But he does not find forgetfulness. And love once more leads him by its irresistible hand back to the door of his beloved.

He knocks again. She asks, "Who is there?" Still confident, he replies, "It is I." She again tells him to go away, but this time she adds this mysterious phrase, "You are not telling me the one word which will let me open to you."

Indignant, distraught, yet intrigued, he goes away again. Not however to look for forgetfulness in faraway travels, but rather to live in solitude and enter deep into meditation. The anger and passion little by little give way to wisdom. His love gains in depth what it loses in violence, and after many, many years it leads him back to the door of his beloved.

The young man—timid, humble and more fervent than ever—knocks discreetly. "Who is there?" she asks. In a quiet voice, he answers, "It is you." At once, his beloved opens the door.[25]

CHAPTER FIVE:
GOLDEN FLOWER

In him was life, and the life was the light of men. The light shines in the darkness, and the darkness has not overcome it.

John 1:4-5

All living creatures are sparks from the radiation of God's brilliance, and these sparks emerge from God like the rays of the sun....If God did not give off these sparks, how would the divine flame become fully visible?
Hildegard of Bingen,
Scivias: The Book of Divine Works

I knew that this little light [of my dream] was my consciousness....Though infinitely small and fragile in comparison with the powers of darkness, it is still a light....My task was to shield the light and not look back.
C. G. Jung, Memories, Dreams, Reflections

At the center of our being is a point of nothingness, a point or spark which belongs entirely to God....It is in everybody and if we could see it we would see these billions of points of light coming together in the face and blaze of a sun.
Thomas Merton, Conjectures of a Guilty Bystander

The flower above my desk is a double buttercup.
I found it in the darkness deep within my heart.

Golden Flower
(Prose Poem)

I sit at my desk and look at the photo of the golden flower. The flower is round like the sun, the moon, the earth. Innumerable cup-shaped petals cluster around the center. They open ever so slightly. Deep yellow spills over my desk, onto my journal. For but an instant I hold gold in my hands.

When I was a child, I looked for magic buttercups in the fields. I would pick the most perfect ones, with smooth petals and long stems. I'd place the flower close to my skin, to my wrist or my arm. If the deep yellow color were reflected, tinting my skin gold, then the buttercup was a magic one. I would hurry back home, carrying my little flower like a chalice.

The flower above my desk is a double buttercup. I found it in the darkness deep within my heart. The fallow ground needed to be broken. The roots needed water, the leaves needed light. But there it grew and there it remains, a flower on God's altar.

I dreamed once of this golden flower. The dream was warm and comforting. It followed a terrifying, turbulent dream in which I am trying to make peace between two ancient enemies, like two gods. I am the housekeeper of one of them, the god of day. Across the way is his enemy, the god of night. Once, as we are sitting at the table, I see the god of night closing his house to leave. I call to him. He turns but continues on his way. I call again, telling him to come. He and my host have been enemies too long. He stops and listens. I open the door. My host tries to stop me. He doesn't want the giant of night at his table. There is a terrible scene. The two giants go after each other. The walls tremble. I try to stop my host. He lets go of the giant of night and turns on me, forcing me backward, pinning me down, as if to bite my neck.

I woke up in deep fright. I was caught between the two giants. Between day and night. Between light and darkness. I wanted them to live in peace with each other. These are ancient enemies, not easily reconcilable. The dream reflected my Judeo-Christian tradition, which sets the two forces in opposition. I felt powerless to bring them together. I was pinned to the ground.

Then shortly afterward, in a second dream, I am living in a large old house, with my husband and children. There is an open courtyard in the middle of the house. Among the many guests is a stranger, a man who loves me. He has given me a bouquet of beautiful yellow flowers that I have put in my bedroom. The guests stay for the night. In the early hours the man comes to my room to give me a kiss on the side of my neck.

Where he kissed me was the same place on my neck where the giant was ready to bite me. I was no longer immobile, pinned to the ground. I felt healed from my battle with the giant of day. I was free. Free to be with either day or night, free to be with both. When I wrote down the dream, I could still see the yellow flowers. I sketched one of the blossoms. It was not a flower I knew. Deep yellow, full of little petals, very round. It made me think of the flower in an ancient Taoist text about meditation, *The Secret of the Golden Flower*. In offering me the golden flower, the unknown guest of my dream was revealing the secret. In reconciling the giants of night and day, he was showing me that opposites could be brought together, darkness and light, yin and yang—the two forces of the Tao—female and male.

I remembered reading *The Secret of the Golden Flower*, not an easy book, but an illuminating one along my path of prayer, letting me better understand and appreciate my longing for darkness. I had lived too much in the light, taking care of my giant of day. I had grown up in a light-filled world, in a society where darkness is an unlived shadow. Everything was to be out in the open, filled with sunshine and smiles. That which was broken was thrown away. That which was ugly was hidden away. And that which was unexplainable was brushed away. There was no other side. There was no room for darkness, for mystery. Surely this had been part of the attraction of studying philosophy, where sometimes there are no answers. Of becoming Catholic, where the numinous is sacramental. Of moving to Europe, the dark continent, and of marrying Pierre, so very much the other. My soul needed the night.

This eighth-century Chinese alchemical text describes how light can be kindled in darkness, how in meditation the flame of consciousness can be heated and circulated until it crystallizes into the golden flower. The golden flower is the immortal spirit body. It is the symbol of spiritual rebirth.

> This condition is the penetration of heaven into earth, the time when all wonders return to their roots. So it is when the crystallized spirit goes into the space of energy....Then out of the obscure darkness, a something develops from the nothingness, that is, the Golden Flower of the great One appears.
> *The Secret of the Golden Flower*[26]

I saw here the incarnation. I saw the spark of light in each soul catching fire. I saw the *scintillae*, the fiery sparks of light dispersed throughout the creation, illuminating the night. The Gnostic sparks of "the ineffable Light." The sparks in the creation myth related by the Kabbalists where the vessels holding the original light shatter and the light explodes into millions of sparks. In writing this, I am vastly oversimplifying a concept that by moments only my heart, not my head, can grasp. Yet it resonates deep within me. The light which circulates is that which is conscious—my conscious self. When it encounters the dark, that which is unconscious—the unconscious Self—the spark flares up. There is conflagration. And slowly with years of practice, the Golden Flower blossoms.

My golden flower became deeply important for me. I held it in my hands but also in my heart and in my mind. It is the symbol that brings together body, mind and soul. The golden flower of my dream had touched all three. My body was set on fire, kissed by Eros in the dark. My skin tingled, I was alive and animated. My mind was stilled, its oppositions brought together. I was no longer questioning. I was at peace. And my soul was opened. Like a blossom. God was both within and without.

I took my drawing to the flower shop where I found my flower. It was a plant with waxy green leaves and one deep yellow flower—round, with innumerable petals, like a lotus, like the Chinese golden flower. It is called *renoncule* in French. I bought the plant and took it home where I put it on the table in my bedroom as I had put the bouquet of yellow flowers in my dream. Finding the flower and putting it in the same place was a way to honor my dream, a ritual to keep the image of my dream alive.

I looked up *renoncule* in the dictionary to find the English word. *Buttercup*, "a deep yellow flower, the color of butter, with five cup-shaped petals." The plant grows wild. Its leaves are lobed, like the feet of birds, explaining why sometimes the flower is also called crowfoot. Then I looked it up in the encyclopedia and found a picture of the single buttercup, like the ones I used to collect in my childhood and hold close to my skin to see if they were magic, if the yellow coloring were reflected. I turned the page and found a picture of the double buttercup, a round flower with innumerable petals on a long stem. Here was the golden flower of my dream, the same one that was now sitting on the table in my room.

My flower lasted a long time. I took a photo of it and put it on the wall above my desk, next to the little cinquefoil, the one I wrote about earlier in this book, the one I found on the path in New York. That first flower was so light, I didn't know whether it was in my hand or not. It was light like the ashes of my father. The second flower had turned to gold, a round, deep yellow flower with innumerable petals spilling out light. From cinquefoil to the golden flower.

What does all this have to do with the ways of prayer? Let me go back to the first chapter, to the call of darkness in the center of the cinquefoil. My prayer life needed to deepen. I needed to let myself sink into the dark. In chapter 2 the cherry tree was no longer blossoming. It needed water. Likewise my prayer life was searching for water. I needed to find the source of living water within. There follows the story of the pear tree, teaching me to see mandalas of white blossoms in the dark. To rest in the cloud of unknowing, without trying to understand. Then in chapter 4 the crack in the acorn gives birth to the oak tree. So my soul needed to find the crack to open to God. Now in this chapter the dark stranger gives me a golden flower. A symbol of rebirth, of the bringing together of light and darkness.

My prayer life was witnessing the meeting of day and night. In the darkness of my heart, the clarity of God's presence was becoming visible. I wish to tiptoe around this. How is it possible, a light in the depths of darkness? It is unimaginable. A darkness so dark that it is radiant. I put my fingers to my lips. My tongue is silent. The cloud grows transparent. I walk lightly in the dark. Yet my soul rises up like Jacob after the angel blessed him. "And Jacob raised a monument in the place where he had spoken with him, a stone monument, on which he made a libation and poured oil. Jacob named the place Bethel where God had spoken with him" (Genesis 35:14-15). God's house. I am in God's house. I am God's house.

I return for another moment to *The Secret of the Golden Flower*. When Jung first read this text, he saw it as confirmation of his psychological findings that in the psyche—the soul—there is both the conscious and the unconscious. And in the center of the soul there is the essence of the Self. Intrigued by the concepts and language of this Eastern text,

Jung was led into his exhaustive study of Western alchemy. He realized that this archaic form of chemistry, which outwardly sought to turn base metals into gold, was also a meditative practice to find the inner gold. The medieval alchemists were looking for the spark of the Self, the essence of God, which was buried deep within the heart.

In writing about this spark, in seeing the cinquefoil turn into gold, the dark ashes of my father turn into light, I see the alchemist at work. His archaic words for the different steps resonate in my imagination. *Nigredo*, the dark. *Albedo*, the light. *Rubedo*, the gold. I see them as stages in my way of praying. Not necessarily as successive stages, rather as circles of prayer overlapping, sometimes dark, sometimes light, sometimes golden. I move back and forth through them. *Nigredo*, the dark night, the moment of deepening—my need to encounter the dark, to shed my outer self. *Albedo*, the light cast in darkness, a dawning consciousness—my growing awareness of emptiness, the knowing in the cloud of unknowing. And *rubedo*, the congealed light, the new consciousness—seeing white mandalas in the dark, watching the cherry tree blossom anew. Jung called the final goal of transformation, the *coniunctio*, the marriage of opposites. It is the *coniunctio* that produces the philosopher's stone, or in Eastern alchemy and meditation the golden flower.

It was this *coniunctio* that I dreamed about, the bringing together of the giant of day and the giant of night. In the same way that my introduction to Jungian thinking renewed my faith in God, now my work in Jungian analysis was healing the split between my intellect and my intuition, my mind and my heart. I was uniting them. If while living with the giant of day, in the focused light of my intellect, I could invite to his table the giant of night—the more chaotic shadow of my imagination—there would be indeed a marriage of opposites, and the golden flower would be the fruit. It was this *coniunctio* that I was experiencing in my prayer life.

> In the beginning was the Word,
> the Word was with God
> and the Word was God....
> In him was life,
> and the life was the light of men.
> The light shines in the darkness
> and the darkness has not overcome it.
> John, 1:1-5 RSV

"The light shines in the darkness...." The light is God's image within us. When it grows bright, his image grows bright. God is unceasingly being born in all of creation. As Meister Eckhart said, What does God do all day? He gives birth. This is what I see when the dark branch of the cherry tree bursts to life each spring with small buds bursting into white blossoms. So it is in each one of us. God is giving birth within us. And Eckhart asks, preaching one Christmas Eve, what good is it if two thousand years ago, a virgin gave birth to the Christ Child, if we do not give birth to him each day in our souls? "What matters is that it shall happen in me."[27] That God be born in me. This is an astounding statement. How can it happen?

The Eucharist is one way. There God the Father transforms the offering of his Son, and in so doing he transforms our offerings. Like the bread and the wine, we ourselves are transformed. Christ is born within us. The ongoing divinization is fed by the Eucharist. When the priest holds up the Eucharist—the mandala of love—he holds up all of creation. "This is my body." The bread is broken and shared. "This is my blood." The vessel becomes one with its contents. It is this immense mystery that pulled me into the Catholic Church as a young adult and that keeps me anchored there. I go back to Teilhard de Chardin, who wrote, "...a single event has been developing in the world: the Incarnation, realized, in each individual, through the Eucharist."[28] And I participate in this profound mystery. The Incarnation. Christ the medium. The Eucharist the medium. And I the vessel becoming one with its contents. One with God. I leave the church, the little girl who has found the magic buttercup. I carry myself like a chalice, filled with God's presence.

So also does each act of prayer nourish the birth of the sacred. "Be still and know that I am God" (Psalm 46:10). Each moment that I remain still in the presence of God, I am creating a *temenos* where God gives birth. And in so doing I am increasing not only my awareness of his presence, but the world's awareness of his presence. In the language of modern physics, this is called morphic resonance. Something that becomes a habit for me resonates around me and becomes a habit for someone else. Prayer is the expression of our longing for God. As I give expression to this longing, I contribute to its expression in others around me, in others around the world. This contemporary language finds echoes in the writings of our great mystics.

Julian of Norwich, the fourteenth-century mystic and anchoress, wrote that all prayer has the same roots. Shortly after the sixteen "showings" that our Lord gave her all on the same day, she wrote *Revelations of Divine Love*, which she later rewrote into a longer work. God showed her that it was his pleasure and his will that we pray. "He showed this to be true in the lovely words, 'I am the foundation of your praying.'"[29] God is the foundation of our prayer. God is the one ground. Julian writes at length about this "one-ing." It is through prayer that the soul becomes one with God. And it is God, the first to receive our prayer. "He puts it in the treasury where it will never perish. There it remains ever helping our needs."[30] Each of our prayers goes into this treasury of prayer. A treasury of prayer for all the creation. It is like a vast one-ing reaching around the entire world. A huge embrace. God hugging the creation. Each prayer of mine enters this hug, this one-ing.

Just as each act of prayer nourishes this divinization, this one-ing, so does each act of love. Our Lord's words echo. "I was hungry and you gave me food; I was thirsty and you gave me drink; I was a stranger and you made me welcome; naked and you clothed me, sick and you visited me, in prison and you came to see me" (Matthew 25:35-38). I answer and say, But when Lord did I give you food and drink? God answers, "As you did to one of the least of these brothers of mine, you did it to me" (Matthew 25:40). Each little act of love unites— "ones"— me to God. When I look after one of my children, I am looking after Our Lord. When I touch my child's hand, I touch God's hand. Likewise and more difficult, when I look after a stranger, I am looking after Our Lord. When I touch a stranger's hand, I touch God's hand.

Why? Because love is the meaning of all life. The meaning of all creation. Love is our meaning. It is again to Julian that I refer. For more than fifteen years after the showings, she continued to ask Our Lord their meaning. Then in her spirit's understanding, she was answered, "You would know our Lord's meaning in this thing? Know it well. Love was his meaning. Who showed it you? Love. What did he show you? Love. Why did he show it? For love."[31]

From my earliest recollections, I have had intimations of this one-ing. Feeling the oneness of the universe. I was one with the world as it spread out around me in the fields of my childhood. Hugging a maple tree, sitting on my warm rock, playing with my one bosom pal, sitting down to the table with my family, I was part of everything around me. At boarding school, whether in the chapel surrounded by other students or alone in my room, my world was one. My body and spirit were one. I was one with God. So I lived my young adult years. In marriage, this one-ing included Pierre. We sought one another. Together we sought God. Our love song was for one another, as it was for God.

> Set me like a seal on your heart,
> like a seal on your arm.
> For love is as strong as Death
> jealousy relentless as Sheol.
> The flash of it is a flash of fire,
> a flame of Yahweh himself.
> Love no flood can quench,
> no torrents drown.
> Song of Songs, 8:6–7

In this tremendous one-ing, our souls were united in God. And in this one-ing, our love gave birth.

We are one in God. We are one in the Lord. And we are one in the Spirit. The Trinity. My intelligence slowly lets go of trying to understand the three different persons in one. Julian put it very simply, "So when He made us, God almighty was our kindly Father, and God all-wise was our kindly Mother, and the Holy Spirit was their love and goodness; all one God, one Lord."[32] It is in this uniting together that God creates us. God our kindly Father and God our kindly Mother. Extraordinary. The Trinity is the original and the great one-ing. A one-ing so immense that it is ongoing and unending. God forever is giving birth.

The *coniunctio*. In becoming man, God becomes potentially every man and woman. As taught by St. Irenaeus in the second century, "God became man so that man might become God."[33] So that we might become God. It sounds scandalous. How can I write that I become God. I cannot write it. I write instead I become one with God. This I can write. In the depths of prayer, I seem to fade, to vanish. My body is stilled. My mind and imagination are stilled. I no longer feel myself present. I no longer feel. The "I" disappears. There are no images, no words. I the subject am not there. Not there to see any image. Not there to hear any word. Instead God is the subject.

Merton, in *New Seeds of Contemplation*, explains, "For in the depths of contemplative prayer there seems to be no division between subject and object."[34] As long as we experience ourselves in prayer as "I," we are still far from the experience of pure contemplation. When the next step comes—yet Merton says, it is not a step and we do not take it—there is no longer any space between Lover and Beloved. "What happens is that the separate entity that is you apparently disappears and nothing seems to be left but love identified with Love....You are not you, you are fruition."[35] Here, Merton tells us, words fall to pieces. Adjectives are worthless. Metaphor becomes hopeless. It is not my experience. I become experience. Darkness is no longer darkness. Emptiness is no longer emptiness. It is the fruition of God. And Merton concludes, "...contemplation becomes what it is meant to be, it is no longer something infused by God into a created subject, so much as God living in God."[36]

Recently I experienced this wholeness for an instant when I walked the labyrinth at Grace Cathedral in San Francisco. Alone one afternoon, I discovered I was close to the cathedral and decided to visit it. It was the day that a new stone labyrinth in the front courtyard was to be blessed. I accepted this as a gift and prepared to walk it when I saw that the labyrinth was the same as the one I had seen at Chartres Cathedral in France. But at Chartres, it was covered with the chairs for the celebration of Mass. So there, some eight thousand kilometers away, I was walking the labyrinth from Chartres. Following the stone path, I gradually let go of distractions, let go of the burdens that I was still carrying in my arms so far from home. I walked slowly, very much alone. This was like a cleansing, a washing away of my worries. When I reached the center, the bells of the cathedral burst into "Amazing Grace." I caught my breath and stood in deep wonderment.

This experience of wholeness, of mystical union, is imaged in the mandala. At our core is the image of the divine. We are drawn to it. Contemplation moves us inward. We enter the center and sink into its radiant darkness. We breathe in God and become radiant ourselves, lighting a circle around us. Communion moves us outward. We breathe out God. We touch all those around us. Our light kindles their light. Until out of breath, we let the center draw us back. Back to our source. Where all is one.

As I write this, the mandalas overlap. Cinquefoil, cherry tree, pear blossom, acorn, golden flower. When I give writing workshops, showing ways to tap into the resources of our creativity, often I ask the participants to draw mandalas. To take a fresh piece of paper and draw a large circle with a center. I suggest that they place an image in the center, an image that speaks to them, an image from their dreams or from their surroundings. Then they fill up the larger circle with whatever they wish. Where does the image take them? What does it reveal to them? What is in the space around the center? And I ask them to give a name to their mandala.

It's like tossing a pebble into a pond and watching the circles of water ripple out from the center. Each image is a pebble. In looking at my book, each chapter is a story of circles, amplifying the original image. And since the center of each mandala is our one same center — our one same source — all the circles are concentric.

If I draw a mandala of the first image, the cinque-foil, where does it take me? From the ashes of my father back to my childhood. To the fields around the white farmhouse. To the wooden fences that I used to climb. As I draw, I breath in and slowly I breath out. I take my time. I walk along the fences. It is the process that impels my imagination, that takes me deeper into stillness.

A friend shows me how to do a monoprint, placing a piece of paper on a plate of glass coated with black oil paint. With a soft pencil, I draw a circle. I draw the five-petal flower, the cinquefoil in the center. I no longer think about the art work. The petals grow larger, widening like the fields into the horizon. I am walking in them. Where they touch one another, there are spokes. I follow them, like the wooden fences. They turn around the center. I go still farther, circling with them. I reach outward. Then, tired and breathless I return to the center.

My drawing is done.

I turn back to the golden flower. My cinquefoil has been transformed. The simple five-petal flower that grows along my path has become the golden flower of my dream. These images express better than words my experience of prayer. Such images are living symbols, awakening us to a new awareness of the inner meaning of life. True symbols take us to the center of the circle. It is in this center that we enter consciously into contact with our deepest self. It is here that there is the one-ing of the soul and its Creator.

*I draw the five-petal flower, the cinquefoil in the center....The
petals grow larger, widening like the fields into the horizon.*

I draw now a mandala of the golden flower, again in the way of a monoprint. First the outer circle, then the inner circle. I let myself enter into its center. Into the center of the golden flower, where the giant of day meets the giant of night, where the light and the darkness come together. The flower begins to blossom. I draw petals, simple cup-shaped petals around the center. I draw very slowly, circle after circle, ever widening. My breath deepens and reaches outward with each round of petals. I color in the remaining space. I look at the print. It is very dark. I take another piece of paper and catch the negative, the drawing left on the plate of glass. I stop in amazement. A reversal. The dark lines have turned light. The mandala is luminous.

Drawing these mandalas, imaging my cinquefoil and my golden flower, I enter into the center. In this center is the spark. When it catches fire, it lights the darkness. The spark is in everyone's soul. It is the spark of our Creator shining in the dark. This spark is ours to tend, to take care of until it flares into a brilliant flame, lit by the right hand of God. "Listen, I am about to kindle a fire in you that will burn up every green tree as well as every dry one; it will be an unquenchable blaze..." (Ezekiel 20:47).

I do not hear God's voice as Ezekiel did. But day by day, since first keeping company with God, I am drawn to the spark of God's light. I sit still, in silence and in darkness. I tend whatever radiance God kindles. When the spark flares up and catches fire, I become one with the golden flower in the succession of eternities.

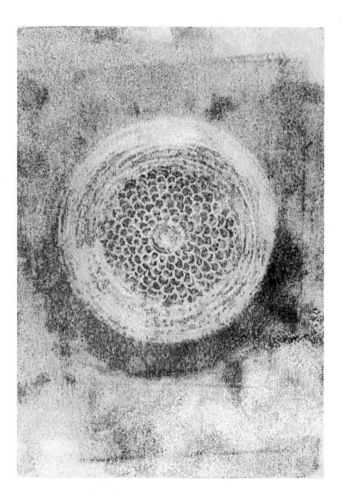

I draw now a mandala of the golden flower...
the light and the darkness come together.

Prayer Mandala

Each way of prayer is unique. Yet, as I close this book, in the spirit with which I wrote it, I offer this example of one way of prayer. May it be an invitation to silence.

First I quiet myself. This can take the form of *lectio divina*, listening to the Scriptures, taking one passage and lingering over it. Or listening to the words of one of our mystics, reading a few pages of *The Cloud of Unknowing*, Saint Teresa of Avila, Thomas Merton and stopping when something kindles a spark within me. Sometimes I get ready for prayer by going for a walk, staying aware of each step while repeating a few words of a psalm, or simply by looking out the window, focusing on the deep green leaves until they glow, or on the brilliant yellow leaves until they are aflame.

Then I am ready to enter into God's presence. I pause and breathe deeply, feeling waves of fresh air move through me. I imagine a circle around me. I draw it in my mind. This is my mandala, with God in the center. I invite my loved ones and the world around me to enter with me into the circle. Sometimes I think of each one, naming them in a litany. Sometimes I include intentions for the world in which I live. Other times I open wide my arms and in one swift embrace I pull them all in with me. This gathering does not take but a few minutes.

As I center myself in God's presence, there is a necessary emptying. I am still too much present. I let the distractions come and go, sometimes using one word as a shield, "God," "Jesus," "Mary," "love." Slowly with each breath, I move inward, toward the center of the mandala, into the mystery of God's love. Then again outward. I let go of the distractions, I let go of the shield. And I enter more deeply into the numinous dark center. In and out. My mind, my hands grow lighter. My breathing becomes secondary. Darkness envelops me. Stillness surrounds me. This stillness is not mine. It is God's gift, his love welling up in my heart. It overflows.

This is my prayer. Words and thoughts disappear. There are no images. A centering in God's love. A magnifying of God's presence. Most of the time I rest through sheer will power, believing that prayer is practice. In very rare moments, the spark of God's presence flares in the dark. The "I" disappears. There is only the Other.

Notes

1. Thomas Merton, *Conjectures of a Guilty Bystander* (Garden City, N.Y.: Doubleday, 1966), p. 146.

2. Meister Eckhart, *Meister Eckhart from Whom God Hid Nothing* (Boston: Shambhala, 1996), p. 48.

3. Thomas Merton, *The Collected Poems of Thomas Merton* (New York: New Directions, 1977), "The Strange Islands," p. 280.

4. William Shannon, *Silence on Fire* (New York: Crossroads, 1995), Selected Merton Texts, Letter to Abdul Aziz, January 2, 1966, p. 43.

5. Thomas Merton, *Contemplative Prayer* (New York: Herder, 1969), p. 69.

6. John of the Cross, *Dark Night of the Soul* (New York: Doubleday Image Books, 1990), book 2, chapter 5, p. 100.

7. *John of the Cross*, Wilfrid McGreal, O Carm. (Liguori, Mo.: Triumph, 1996). Text from *The Collected Works of St John of the Cross*, translated by Kieran Kavanaugh and Otilio Rodriguez, stanzas 1 and 3, pp. 28-29.

8. Thomas Merton, *Way of Chuang Tzu* (New York: New Directions, 1965), reading 12, 4, Chuang Tzu, retold by Thomas Merton, p. 74.

9. Teresa of Avila, *The Interior Castle* (New York: Doubleday, 1989), "Fourth Mansion," p. 81.

10. Ibid., "Sixth Mansion," p. 158.

11. Ibid., "Fifth Mansion," p. 96.

12. Pierre Teilhard de Chardin, *Hymn of the Universe* (New York: Harper & Row, 1965), "Mass on the World," p. 20.

13. Thomas Merton, *Seven Storey Mountain* (New York: Harcourt Brace, 1948), p. 260.

14. Henri Caffarel, *Lettres sur la prière* (Paris: Editions Feu Nouveau, 1960), "La légende de chevrotin," translator Susan Tiberghien, p. 84.

15. Raissa Maritain, *Journal de Raissa* (Paris: Desclée de Brouwer, 1963), editor Jacques Maritain, translator Susan Tiberghien, p. 306.

16. Ibid., p. 83.

17. Ibid., p. 211.

18. *Cloud of Unknowing* (Mahwah, N.J.: Paulist Press, 1981), chapter 3, p. 120.

19. Ibid., chapter 5, p. 128.

20. Ibid., chapter 68, p. 252.

21. Ibid., chapter 5, p. 128.

22. Thomas Merton, *Conjectures of a Guilty Bystander,* p. 156.

23. *Cloud of Unknowing,* chapter 68, pp. 251-52.

24. John Neihardt, *Black Elk Speaks* (Lincoln: University of Nebraska, 1979), "The Great Vision," pp. 42-43. When

Neihardt asked Black Elk where the vision took place, he replied it was on top of Harney Peak in the Black Hills. "But anywhere is the center of the world."

25. Henri Caffarel, *Lettres sur la prière,* "C'est toi," translator Susan Tiberghien, pp. 143-44.

26. Richard Wilhelm, translator, *The Secret of the Golden Flower* (New York: Harcourt Brace Jovanovich, 1931), pp. 56, 61.

27. Meister Eckhart, *Meister Eckhart from Whom God Hid Nothing,* p. 45.

28. Pierre Teilhard de Chardin, *The Divine Milieu* (New York: Harper & Row, 1965), part 3, p. 124.

29. Julian of Norwich, *Revelations of Divine Love* (London: Penguin, 1966), "Fourteenth Showing," chapter 41, p. 124.

30. Ibid., "Fourteenth Showing," chapter 41, p. 124.

31. Ibid., "Sixteenth Showing," chapter 86, p. 211.

32. Ibid., "Fourteenth Showing," chapter 58, p. 165.

33. Quotation generally attributed to St. Irenaeus, Bishop of Lyons (c. 130-200). Evelyn Underhill (*Mysticism* [New York: Penguin, 1974], p. 410) attributed it to St. Athanasius, *De Incarn.Verbi,* i, 108.

34. Thomas Merton, *New Seeds of Contemplation* (New York: New Directions, 1962), chapter 36, p. 267.

35. Ibid., chapter 38, p. 283.

36. Ibid., chapter 38, p. 284.

Suggested Readings

This is not an exhaustive list, but rather suggestions of books that have helped me find my way in silent prayer. I share these titles as I would with a friend.

The Classics of the Christian Tradition
(chronological order)

The Holy Bible. The quotations I have used come from the Jerusalem Bible (London: Darton, Longman & Todd, the Popular Edition, 1974), except for the psalms, which are from the Revised Standard Version (New York: Thomas Nelson and Sons, 1952). A few exceptions are marked with the letters JB or RSV.

The Philokalia. "The Love of Good" — collected wisdom of the desert fathers, including texts on prayer and spiritual life written between the fourth and fifteenth centuries by spiritual masters of the Orthodox Christian tradition.
   Writings from the Philokalia on Prayer of the Heart. Translated by E. Kadloubovsky, and G. E. H. Palmer. London: Faber and Faber Limited, 1951. Selected texts on contemplative stillness and union with God.

Hildegard of Bingen (1098-1179), Rhineland mystic — poet, musician, healer, artist, prophet, and abbess of a Benedictine Abbey — whose written testimony of her visions blends divine inspiration with keen human intellect. Her work, which influenced thousands during her lifetime, is again awakening thousands to a deeper mystical awareness.

Illuminations of Hildegard of Bingen. Santa Fe: Bear and Company, 1985. Text by Hildegard of Bingen with commentary by Matthew Fox. A beautiful introduction, with clear commentary. The pictures of her illuminations give an almost contemporary presentation to medieval iconography.

Hildegard von Bingen's Mystical Visions. Translated by Bruce Hozeski. Santa Fe: Bear and Company, 1986. Formerly titled *Scivias* (Know Thy Ways). Here we have Hildegard's answer to God's request, "Write what you see and hear! Tell people how to enter the kingdom of salvation!" Includes the musically set drama *Ordo Virtutum.*

Hildegard of Bingen's Book of Divine Works, with Letters and Songs. Edited by Matthew Fox. Santa Fe: Bear and Company, 1987. Contains major portions of *De Operation Dei,* the final work in her cosmological trilogy, plus the most significant of her letters, sermons, poems, and songs.

Meister Eckhart (1260–1329), the German Dominican priest whose writings form an essential part of the foundation of the Western mystical tradition and whose popular preachings brought him under scrutiny of church authorities. His central tenet held that the germ of God lies within all His creatures.

Meister Eckhart from Whom God Hid Nothing. Edited by David O'Neal. Boston: Shambhala, 1996. Brings together short fragments with longer treatises and sermons, to serve as an introduction to the writing of one of the greatest medieval European mystics.

Meister Eckhart, Selected Writings. Selected and translated by Oliver Davies. London: Penguin Books, 1994.

Confirms Eckhart's position in Christian mysticism and theology, highlighting how he sought to reconcile tenets of Neoplatonism and traditional Christian belief.

Meister Eckhart, The Essential Sermons, Commentaries, Treatises, and Defense. Mahwah, N.J.: Paulist Press, 1981. In the Classics of Western Spirituality series, this volume presents Eckhart's technical Latin writings along with the more accessible German sermons and treatises. Preface by Huston Smith and introduction by Edmund Colledge and Bernard McGinn.

Julian of Norwich (1342-1415), anchoress, living in recluse in Norwich, wrote one book twice, *The Sixteen Revelations of Divine Love*, describing the showings that appeared to her May 8, 1373. The precision of her theology, depth of her insight, and simplicity of her expression are revealed in the often quoted teaching, "Sin is necessary but all shall be well and all shall be well."

Revelations of Divine Love. London: Penguin Books, 1966. An account of the revelations that continues to inspire spiritual seekers six centuries later. An amazing and appealing mystical treatise.

Author unknown. *The Cloud of Unknowing.* Edited by James Walsh, S.J. Mahwah, N.J.: Paulist Press, 1981. Important volume in the Classics of Western Spirituality, with preface by Simon Tugwell, O.P., and introduction by James Walsh, S.J.. Written by an anonymous English monk during the late fourteenth century to instruct a younger monk in the contemplative method of prayer. It teaches an approach to God through darkness (the apophatic way), through unknowing, in the tradition of Gregory of Nyssa (fourth century).

Teresa of Avila (1515-91), Spanish Carmelite mystic, reformer of religious life in the Carmelite order, incredibly gifted teacher, inspiring her sisters and, through her writings, her readers to participate in the mystical search for the ultimate spiritual reality.
   The Interior Castle. New York: Image Book, Doubleday, 1989. Widely read book on mystical theology, guiding souls toward spiritual perfection. The central image is that of the soul as passing through many rooms of a castle of many rooms before reaching communion with God in the center.

St. John of the Cross (1542-91), St. Teresa's greatest disciple, poet, philosopher and contemplative, whose verse and prose works form a sublime spiritual canticle. His writings witness the flowering of Divine grace in the life of this Spanish Carmelite.
   Dark Night of the Soul. New York: Image Book, Doubleday, 1990. In the continuation of *Ascent of Mount Carmel*, St. John of the Cross recounts here the journey of the soul upon the spiritual road to perfect union of love with God. This great composite work gives illustration to the truth that grace ennobles nature and reveals the essential harmony between the natural and the supernatural.

Merton, Thomas (1915-68), spiritual master, Trappist monk, writer, and peace activist, came to international prominence with his classic autobiography, *The Seven Storey Mountain*, and over the rest of his life (tragically ended in Bangkok at the age of 53), he achieved authentic communion through his prodigious writing. His life embodied the quest for God and for human solidarity in the contemporary world. Here follows (in chronological order of publication) only some of his over sixty books, not counting pamphlets, works edited by others, and journals and letters, still being published.

The Seven Storey Mountain. New York: Harcourt, Brace, 1948. An introduction to Thomas Merton, the story of his early life and spiritual conversion, up to his first years at the Trappist Monastery of Our Lady of Gethsemani, containing the themes he would later deepen, including his deep concept of God as Being Itself. Merton himself later criticized in his early writing a romantic approach to monastic life.

Selected Poems. New York: New Directions, 1959. Enlarged edition, 1967. Merton was not only a prominent Catholic poet, but also one of the most vital American poets of his time, giving a lyrical voice to the spiritual quest of contemporary man.

New Seeds of Contemplation. New York: New Directions, 1962. Enlarged, revised version of *Seeds of Contemplation* (1948), placing Merton in the contemplative tradition of St. John of the Cross, the medieval mystics, and *The Cloud of Unknowing.* Awakens reader to the inner depths of the spirit.

The Way of Chuang Tzu. New York: New Directions, 1965. Working from existing translations, Merton wrote his personal versions of many readings of Chuang Tzu, the Chinese sage of the fourth century B.C.

Raids on the Unspeakable. New York: New Directions, 1966. Collection of Merton's prose writings, covering themes from the myths of Prometheus to the plays of Ionesco, expressing his militant concern with the situation of humankind in today's world.

Conjectures of a Guilty Bystander. Garden City, N.Y.: Doubleday, 1966. Journal entries, meditations and reflections revealing Merton's love of nature and of the human community. The experiences of a deeply prayerful person.

Mystics and Zen Masters. New York: Farrar, Straus, 1967. Wide-ranging study of different aspects of both Christian tradition and Eastern tradition, aimed to understanding ways in which humanity is led to religious awareness.

Zen and the Birds of Appetite. New York: New Directions, 1968. Essays introducing the reader to Zen as a "trans-cultural, trans-religious, trans-formed consciousness," which Merton believes is part of an authentic creative and spiritual experience.

Contemplative Prayer. New York: Herder, 1969. Brings together a wealth of meditative and mystical influences, from John of the Cross to Eastern desert monasticism, creating a spiritual path where contemplation and action are fused into one entity.

What Is Contemplation? Springfield, Ill.: Templegate Publishers, 1981. Includes the basics of Christian contemplation, guiding the reader into the practice of contemplation. With drawings by the author.

Thoughts on the East. New York: New Directions, 1995. Ecumenical anthology of Merton's essential definitions of Taoism, Buddhism (in many forms, especially Zen), Sufism and Hinduism, unified by his belief that East and West share "a common spiritual climate."

The Asian Journal of Thomas Merton. New York: New Directions, 1973. A mosaic of Asian images and experiences, sacred and profane, recording the beginning of this fateful journey to the Orient, the depth of his spiritual awareness, up to his tragic accidental death, December 10, 1968.

Turning Toward the World: The Journals of Thomas Merton, Volume Four, 1960-63. San Francisco: Harper, 1996. Springing from three hundred handwritten pages that capture the growing unrest of the 1960s, Merton documents his movement from the cloister toward the world. *Dancing in the Water of Life: The Journals of Thomas Merton, Volume Five, 1963-65.* San Francisco: Harper, 1997. At fifty years old, Merton strives for inner peace, spending more time at his hermitage at the Abbey of Gethsemani.

Learning to Love: The Journals of Thomas Merton, Volume Six, 1966-67. San Francisco: Harper, 1997. Merton recommits himself to his vocation as a monk, with a renewed and stronger understanding of both worldly and spiritual love.

Thomas Merton: Spiritual Master: The Essential Writings. Edited by Lawrence S. Cunningham. Mahwah, N.J.: Paulist Press, 1992. Insightful, comprehensive introduction to Merton as monk, theologian, writer, social critic and spiritual master, and a reference book of his most important texts.

Teilhard de Chardin, Pierre (1881-1955), scientist-priest-man of prayer who in poetic language communicates his reverence for the earth and his awareness of the spiritual: of God's presence throughout the created world.

Hymn of the Universe. New York: Harper & Row, 1965. In this most mystical of his works, Teilhard presents his vision of the cosmic Christ and man's union with God.

The Divine Milieu. New York: Harper & Row, 1960. Following Teilhard's *The Phenomenon of Man,* this testimony is key to the mystical understanding of man's role in the universe in collaboration with its ongoing creation.

The Classics of Other Traditions
(chronological order)

I Ching or Book of Changes. Translated by Richard Wilhelm with foreword by C. G. Jung. London: Arkana, 1951, 1989. A book of oracles, over five thousand years old, containing the whole of human experience, and a book of wisdom, exploring the unconscious and intuiting the present moment.

Lao Tzu, *Tao Te Ching.* Richard Wilhelm Edition. London: Arkana, Penguin, 1985. Beautiful Chinese classic of mystical reflection on harmony and flow of life, bringing ancient insight into modern ways of thinking and praying.

The Bhagavad Gita. Translated by Juan Mascaro. London: Penguin Books, 1962. Written about 500 B.C., this masterpiece of Sanskrit literature is the immortal song *(gita)* of the soul's surrender to and awareness of Krishna (the conditioned form of Brahma). Its three themes are love, light and life.

The Secret of the Golden Flower: A Chinese Book of Life. Translated by Richard Wilhelm with commentary by C. G. Jung. New York: Harcourt Brace Jovanovich, 1931, revised edition 1962. Alchemical and meditative Taoist text discovered and translated by Richard Wilhelm, published with part of another meditation text, *The Book of Consciousness and Life.*

The Secret of the Golden Flower. Authoritative new translation by Thomas Cleary. San Francisco: HarperCollins,

1991. Cleary makes this mystical text still more accessible, transcending its cultural setting to reveal its universality.

The Tibetan Book of the Dead: The Great Liberation through Hearing in the Bardo. Boston: Shambhala, 1987. Classic Buddhist scripture, traditionally read aloud to the dying (to help them along the path of liberation), helpful in any situation necessitating transformation.

The Essential Rumi. Translations by Coleman Barks. San Francisco: Harper, 1994. Collection of writings of thirteenth-century giant of Sufi literature and one of the finest spiritual poets of all times, brings alive the soul's yearning to return toward God. Testimony to Rumi's friendship with Shams of Tabriz.

Contemporary Studies and Interpretations (alphabetical order)

Armstrong, Karen. *A History of God: the 4,000-Year Quest of Judaism, Christianity and Islam*. New York: Ballantine Books, 1993. Articulate and learned study of the three dominant monotheistic religions, addressing the question, does the word *God* have meaning today?

Begg, Ean. *The Cult of the Black Virgin*. London: Arkana, 1985. Lucid, comprehensive investigation of the phenomenon of Black Virgins, from their pagan origins to their modern resurfacing.

Bergson, Henri. *The Two Sources of Morality and Religion.* New York: Doubleday, 1954. First published in France in 1932, presents Bergson's concept of creative evolution and his appreciation of mysticism as the expression of the life force enabling our discovery of a human community.

Bolen, Jean Shinoda. *The Tao of Psychology: Synchronicity and the Self.* New York: Harper & Row, 1982. Illuminating study of the important links between psychology and mysticism, the individual and the external world, bridging Eastern and Western thinking.

Bryant, Christopher. *Jung and the Christian Way.* San Francisco: Harper & Row, 1983. Member of an Anglican community, Father Bryant gives enlightening introduction to Jung's thought, based on conviction that it can guide Christians into a deeper experience of the presence of God and Christ.

Caffarel, Henri. *Lettres sur la prière.* Paris: Editions du Feu Nouveau, 1960. A later edition was translated: *Being Present to God: Letters on Prayer*, Alba House, 1983. Gathers together many of Father Caffarel's letters to different correspondents, giving essential glimpses into the practice of contemplation.

Campbell, Joseph. *Myths to Live By.* New York: Viking Penguin, 1972. Written by the author of *The Masks of God*; examines the myths we live by and how they can extend our human and spiritual potential.

   The Inner Reaches of Outer Space, Metaphor as Myth and as Religion. New York: Harper & Row, 1988. Treats the mythic motifs that are common to the religious traditions of humankind and which Jung called the "archetypes of the collective unconscious."

Capra, Fritjof. *The Tao of Physics.* London: HarperCollins, 1976. Classic exploration of connections between Eastern mysticism and modern physics; describes paradigm shift in Western spirituality to a more holistic worldview.

Crowley, Vivianne. *Jungian Spirituality.* London: Thorsons, 1998. Relates Jung's spiritual journey through Eastern traditions, the occult and Christianity to a religious vision for the new millennium, focusing on the development of a spiritual consciousness.

Dourley, John P. *The Illnesses That We Are: A Jungian Critique of Christianity.* Toronto: Inner City Books, 1984. Comprehensive exploration of Jung's appreciation of Christian symbols and ritual, revealing both the strengths and the weaknesses of the Christian myth.
   Love, Celibacy, and the Inner Marriage. Toronto: Inner City Books, 1987. Six essays on Jung's impact on theology, including "Jung and Mechtilde of Magdeburg," "Jung and Tillich" and "Jung's Understanding of Mysticism."

Edinger, Edward F. *The Creation of Consciousness.* Toronto: Inner City Books, 1984. Using religious texts, mythology, concepts of depth psychology, Edinger presents a creative collaboration of the scientific pursuit of knowledge and the religious search for meaning.
   The Mysterium Lectures: A Journey Through C. G. Jung's Mysterium Coniunctionis. Toronto: Inner City Books, 1995. Edinger works his way through Jung's opus, illuminating the alchemical operations and Jung's psychological inter-

pretations. A guide to what is going on in the laboratory of the unconscious and its implications on the soul.

Eliot, T. S. *Four Quartets*. New York: Harcourt Brace, 1943. Eliot leads us to the unmoved center of life, to the still point, where, with echoes of Julian of Norwich, "all shall be well and all manner of thing shall be well."

Estés, Clarissa Pinkola. *Women Who Run with the Wolves: Myths and Stories of the Wild Woman Archetype*. New York: Ballantine Books, 1995. Rooted in family rites, psychology and myth, this book of wisdom awakens the reader to a deeper knowing of the soul.

Flinders, Carol Lee. *Enduring Grace: Living Portraits of Seven Women Mystics*. San Francisco: Harper, 1993. Offers a compelling introduction to the lives, convictions and wisdom of seven European mystics, from Saint Claire of Assisi (thirteenth century) to Saint Thérèse of Lisieux (nineteenth century).

Fox, Matthew. *Original Blessing: A Primer in Creation Spirituality*. Santa Fe: Bear and Company, 1983. Presents creation-centered tradition (against the fall/redemption tradition) as fourway path (*via positiva, via negativa, via creativa, via transformativa*) to a spiritual awakening for the contemporary world.

　　Natural Grace: Dialogues on Creation, Darkness, and the Soul in Spirituality and Science. Coauthored with Rupert Sheldrake. New York: Doubleday, 1996. Imaginative approach to the recognition that a synthesis between science and spirituality is not only possible but vital.

Gibran, Kahlil. *The Prophet.* New York: Alfred A. Knopf, 1939. Poet-philosopher-author speaks from a deep reservoir of spirituality, giving expression to the deepest longings and impulses of the human soul.

Gleick, James. *Chaos: Making a New Science.* New York: Penguin Books, 1987. Offers a new way of seeing a pattern where formerly there was only the random, the chaotic. A history of discovery to the inner rhythms of creation.

Gustafson, Fred. *The Black Madonna.* Boston: Sigo Press, 1990. Beginning with the history of the Black Madonna of Einsiedeln, this psychological study sheds light on the unconscious archetype of the feminine.

Hanh, Thich Nhat. *Living Buddha, Living Christ.* Introduction by Elaine Pagels. New York: Riverhead Books, 1995. Renowned Buddhist monk explores the spiritual crossroads where traditions of Christianity and Buddhism meet.

Hillman, James. *The Dream and the Underworld.* New York: Harper & Row, 1979. Relates our dream life to the myths of the Underworld, to the dark side of the soul, and re-visions dream interpretation in relation to life and death.

Hirshfield, Jane. *Women in Praise of the Sacred: 43 Centuries of Spiritual Poetry by Women.* New York: HarperCollins, 1994. Anthology of women's spirituality containing unexpected, luminous poems of seventy spiritual teachers and mothers, from a Sumerian moon priestess to Sub-ok of Korea.

James, William. *Varieties of Religious Experience*. New York: Random House, Modern Library Edition, 1994. Classic study in the psychology of religion (1902), discusses conversion, repentance and mysticism. Posits that religious experiences rather than religious tenets are the backbone of religious life.

Jung, C. G. *Memories, Dreams, Reflections*. Recorded and edited by Aniela Jaffé. London: Fontana, 1967, 1983. A unique document of our time, reflecting Jung's humility and his passion to unearth truth. The prophet in Jung stretches the reader's imagination to the confines of creation.

Man and His Symbols. Conceived and edited by Carl Jung. London: Picador, 1964. With collaboration of M.-L. von Franz, Joseph Henderson, Jolande Jacobi, Aniela Jaffé. Five remarkable essays elaborating upon Jung's theory of the significance of symbolism in dreams and art.

Answer to Job in *The Portable Jung*. Edited by Joseph Campbell. New York: Penguin Books, Viking, 1971. Unveils the divine drama between Job and God, leading the reader to come to terms with divine darkness and to deal with its effect. How do we experience God?

Aion: Researches into the Phenomenology of the Self. Princeton: Princeton University Press, 1959, 1969. One of the major works of Jung's later years, treating the symbolic representation of the psychic totality, the Self, whose historical equivalent is the figure of Christ.

On the Nature of the Psyche. Princeton: Princeton University Press, 1960. Comprising two of eighteen essays in volume 8 of the Collected Works, presents an extensive review of Jung's examination of the psyche, the soul and the concepts of consciousness and the unconscious.

The Gnostic Jung. Edited by Robert Segal. Princeton: Princeton University Press, 1992. Presents Jung's main discussions of this ancient form of spirituality, which Jung saw as a prefiguration to his analytical psychology. *Jung's Challenge to Contemporary Religion.* Edited by Murray Stein. Wilmette, Ill.: Chiron, 1987. Remarkable collection of essays extending Jung's thought about modernity, depth psychology and religious experience.

Keating, Thomas. *Open Mind, Open Heart.* Rockport, Mass.: Element Books, 1986. Presents the contemplative practice of centering prayer, replacing contemplative prayer in church history, where during the first sixteen centuries it remained the goal of Christian spirituality.

Luke, Helen M. *The Way of Woman: Awakening the Perennial Feminine.* New York: Doubleday, 1995. Distills a long life's work, applying religion, mythology and literature to the lives of women, reflecting on their sources of spiritual nourishment.

Mallasz, Gitta. *Talking with Angels: A Document from Hungary.* English rendition by Robert Hinshaw. Einsiedeln, Switzerland: Daimon Verlag, 1988, third edition 1998. "I am merely the scribe of the angels," says Gitta Mallasz. Their message puts us in touch with "Truth" and enables us to view the world with Gitta's eyes.

Maritain, Raissa. *Journal de Raissa.* Published by Jacques Maritain. Paris: Desclée de Brouwer, 1963. Translated as *Raissa's Journal,* but out of print. Journals of an extraordinary soul of our century, sharing with us the fruits of contemplation in a world of scholarship and spirituality.
    Les Grandes Amitiés. Brussels: Desclée de Brouwer, 1956. (Not translated.) Beautiful memoir, focusing on the

friendships that surrounded Raissa Maritain during her years at the Sorbonne and her marriage to Jacques.

Moore, Thomas. *Care of the Soul: A Guide for Cultivating Depth and Sacredness in Everyday Life.* New York: Harper-Collins, 1992. By not separating psychology from religion, Moore gives us a handbook for finding meaning in modern day life by nurturing the soul.

Mott, Michael. *The Seven Mountains of Thomas Merton.* Boston: Houghton Mifflin, 1984. This authorized biography takes the title image from Dante, used by Merton for his own autobiography *The Seven Storey Mountain.* Leads the reader through the tumultuous landscape of Merton's life, where underneath lay the quest for the source of all being.

Neihardt, John G. *Black Elk Speaks.* Lincoln: University of Nebraska Press, 1979. Black Elk imparted his life story and that of the Oglala Sioux to his biographer, Neihardt, offering eloquent visions of the unity of all creation.

Norris, Kathleen. *Dakota: A Spiritual Geography.* Boston, Houghton Mifflin, 1993. Poet Norris, evoking the Great Plains, gives us an inspiring and open book of stories and prayer. A gift of hope to her readers.
    The Cloister Walk. New York: Riverhead Books, 1996. Continues author's journey as a poet, believer and married Protestant, compressing years of experience into the diary of one liturgical year at St. John's Abbey, Minnesota.

Nouwen, Henri J. M. *The Way of the Heart.* New York: Ballantine Books, 1981. Based on the spirituality of the desert fathers, Nouwen's simple words about solitude, silence and prayer guide the reader into the love of God.

Odajnyk, Walter. *Gathering the Light: A Psychology of Meditation.* Boston: Shambhala, 1993. Integrative study of ancient and modern wisdom, applying insights of Jungian psychology to meditation, showing how Zen enlightenment compares with Jung's state of "wholeness."

O'Donohue, John. *Anam Cara: Spiritual Wisdom from the Celtic World.* London: Bantam Press, 1997. Irish poet and scholar draws from the spiritual heritage of the Celts and Druids to lead us to a place where our heart can be nourished and where we find our *anam cara,* our soul friend.

Pagels, Elaine. *The Gnostic Gospels.* New York: Vintage Books, Random House, 1989. Brilliant study drawing on the Gnostic Christian texts discovered at Nag Hammadi, Egypt, in 1945. Illuminates the beliefs of the first Christians.

Peck, M. Scott. *The Road Less Traveled.* New York: Simon & Schuster, 1979. Integrates traditional psychological and spiritual insights to lead us along the path to greater serenity and fullness in our contemporary lives.

Pennington, Basil. *Thomas Merton, Brother Monk.* San Francisco: Harper, 1987. Discerning exploration of Merton's life, written with spiritual intellect from inside his community. Pennington, a Cistercian monk, knew Merton well and draws the reader into Merton's spirituality.

Powell, James N. *The Tao of Symbols.* New York: Quill, 1982. A cross-cultural study with rich insights into how symbolic vision expressed in poetry and meditation opens our thinking to new realms.

Rahner, Karl, S.J. *On Prayer*. New York: Deus Books, Paulist Press, 1968. Echoing Saint Augustine's words, "Thou has made us for Thyself, O Lord, and our heart is restless until it rests in Thee," Karl Rahner restates the essential lessons regarding prayer.

Rilke, Rainer Maria. *Letters to a Young Poet*. New York: Norton & Company, 1934, 1954. Timeless, containing precious advice about poetry, love and God, "the coming one, imminent from eternity."

Rinpoche, Sogyal. *The Tibetan Book of Living and Dying*. San Francisco: Harper, 1994. Manual for life and death, and source of sacred inspiration from the heart of the Tibetan tradition, with teachings on meditation, the nature of the mind, compassion, karma and rebirth.

Roberts, Bernadette. *The Experience of No-Self: A Contemplative Journey*. Boston: Shambhala, 1982. A significant personal account of a woman's spiritual path (a Catholic nun for ten years), to high stages of contemplation, into the realm of the Unknown.

Scholem, Gershom. *Major Trends in Jewish Mysticism*. New York: Schocken Books, Random House, 1954, 1995. Scholem, professor of Jewish mysticism at the Hebrew University of Jerusalem until his death in 1982, brings an awareness of Jewish mysticism, along with Jewish history, to this thorough study of Hasidism, Kabbalism, the Zohar and "the living Torah."

Shannon, William H. *Silence on Fire: The Prayer of Awareness.* New York: Crossroad, 1995. An inspiring guide to developing our inner lives through prayer with carefully selected texts from Thomas Merton. *Thomas Merton's Dark Path: The Inner Experience of a Contemplative.* New York: Penguin Books, 1982. A study of the apophatic way through darkness to light in Merton's spirituality. Includes texts from *The Inner Experience,* a work Merton did not wish to be published separately.

Singer, June. *Seeing through the Visible World: Jung, Gnosis, and Chaos.* San Francisco: Harper & Row, 1990. Gives a Jungian-transpersonal perspective on mystical experience and its relationship to everyday reality. Looks at how the invisible world is viewed by scientific and spiritual disciplines.

Suzuki, D. T. *Zen Buddhism: Selected Writings.* Edited by William Barrett. New York: Doubleday, 1956, 1996. Presents background and overview of Zen philosophy and practice. D. T. Suzuki (1869–1966) was the first to open the West to Buddhism. His penetrating writings attracted thinkers such as C. G. Jung, Aldous Huxley and Thomas Merton.

Suzuki, Shunryu. *Zen Mind, Beginner's Mind.* New York: Weatherhill, 1970, 1991. Presents informal talks on how to practice Zen, drawn from centuries of Zen Buddhism and from Dogen, one of the most important Zen masters. An inspiring guide to realizing our true nature.

Tiberghien, Susan M. *Looking for Gold, A Year in Jungian Analysis.* Einsiedeln, Switzerland: Dalmon Verlag 1995, new edition 1997. This book of dreams and reflections recounts the author's deepening of faith and learning to see with her eyes closed.

Ulanov, Ann and Barry. *Transforming Sexuality: The Archetypal World of Anima and Animus.* Boston: Shambala, 1994. Opens the way to deeper self-knowledge and spiritual transformation through a better understanding of the Feminine and the Masculine within ourselves.

Underhill, Evelyn. *Mysticism.* New York: Penguin, Meridian Books, 1974, First Edition, 1910. Classic study of the nature and development of man's spiritual consciousness. Part 1 deals with The Mystic Fact, the historical and explanatory; part 2 with The Mystic Way, the inner process of mystical experience leading to the Unitive Life.

van der Post, Laurens. *Yet Being Someone Other.* London: Penguin, 1982. Episodes of autobiography, revealing van der Post's belief that "in the deeps, all men are already brothers...and that all cultures are tributaries of one great river seeking the same sea of truth" (p. 335).
Jung and the Story of Our Time. London: Penguin, 1976. The story of these two extraordinary men, with a portrait of Jung's creative genius and his lifelong study of man's psyche, of man's soul.

von Franz, Marie-Louise. *Shadow and Evil in Fairy Tales.* Dallas: Spring Publications, 1974. Lectures of von Franz, collaborator with C. G. Jung, examining the depths of archetypal darkness through motifs and symbols of fairy tales.
Alchemy, An Introduction to the Symbolism and the Psychology. Toronto: Inner City Books, 1980. Offers fasci-

nating account of the alchemists' search for inner balance and wholeness and what it can teach the reader.

The Way of a Pilgrim. Translated by Helen Bacovcin, with a foreword by Walter J. Ciszek, S.J. New York: Image Books, Doubleday, 1978, 1992. This anonymous narrative of a Russian Pilgrim retraces the history of the Jesus Prayer (the prayer of the heart) from the Gospels through the *Philocalia* to this nineteenth-century text of a spiritual wayfarer.

Weil, Simone. *Waiting for God*. New York: Harper Perennial, 1992. Meditations on the relationship of our daily lives to the realm of the transcendent, with insights into prayer which she describes as "fixed attention," and into the implicit love of God.

Welch, John, O.Carm. *Spiritual Pilgrims, Carl Jung and Teresa of Avila*. Mahwah, N.J.: Paulist Press, 1982. Enlightening study of the inner journeys of Jung and Teresa, of their similar understanding of the symbolic in the soul's relationship to its inner depths. Welch invites us to our own journey to God.

Wilber, Ken. *Sense and Soul: Integrating Science and Religion*. New York: Random House, 1998. Builds upon the foundation of a true East/West integration, bringing together the spiritual world of ancient wisdom and the empirical world of modern knowledge.

Woodman, Marion. *Addiction to Perfection*. Toronto: Inner City Books, 1982. Brings to light the archetypal patterns functioning in women and celebrates the integration of body and spirit that lies at the heart of the feminine.

Dancing in the Flames: The Dark Goddess in the Transformation of Consciousness. Coauthored with Elinor Dickson. Boston: Shambhala, 1997. Explores the Dark Goddess, hidden in the human psyche, moving among mythology, psychology and religion.

Wu, John C. H. *Beyond East and West.* New York: Sheed & Ward, 1955. This autobiography of a Chinese philosopher and scholar, fully Christian and fully Chinese (Taoist, Confucian and Zen), comes from a deep understanding of the East and West, and points toward reconciliation.

The Golden Age of Zen: The Classic Work on the Foundation of Zen Philosophy. Introduction by Thomas Merton. New York: Doubleday, 1967, 1975, 1996. Explores the religious history after the meeting of Buddhism with Taoism (sixth century) and the movement's flowering in the successive sages.

Index

Biblical references:
Disciples of Emmaus (Luke 24:31-32), 41
Ezekiel (Ezek 20:47), 110
Jacob (Gen 32:25-26), 55; (Gen 35:14-15), 99
"I am the vine...." (John 15:4-5), 69
"I was hungry...." (Matt 25:35-38), 103
"In the beginning was the Word...." (John 1:1-5), 101
Mary and Martha (Luke 10:38-42), 15-16
Mustard Seed (Matt 13:31-32), 76
Nicodemus (John 3:5), 42
Paul's Letters (1 Cor 15:28), 59; (Gal 2:20), 64; (Eph 4:22), 64
Psalms (139), 10; (23), 12; (46) 17, 102; (62), 63; (98), 89
Samaritan Woman at the Well (John 4:13-14), 31-35
Song of Songs (1:5-6), 87; (8:6-7), 104
Wisdom (Prov 8:30), 87; (Wis 7:7-8), 87
Black Elk, 68
Chuang Tzu, 25
Cloud of Unknowing, The (anonymous), 3, 58-60, 63-64, 66, 76
Eckhart, Meister, 1, 5, 17, 24, 55, 69, 74, 76, 81, 101
Hildegard of Bingen, 69, 76, 91
Irenaeus, 15, 105
John of the Cross, 3, 23, 49, 76-77
Julian of Norwich, 4, 5, 102-4
Jung, C. G., 3, 4, 41, 44, 80-81, 91, 99-100
Lao Tsu, 27
Maritain, Raissa, 56-57

Mechtilde of Magdeburg, 27
Merton, Thomas, 3, 14, 18-19, 22, 27, 39, 65, 77, 91, 105
Proclus, 66
Pseudo Dionysus, 49
Rilke, Rainer Maria, 69
Rumi, 27
Secret of the Golden Flower, The (anonymous), 4, 96, 99
Teilhard de Chardin, 37-38, 102
Teresa of Avila, 3, 32-35, 41-42, 76
Way of the Pilgrim, The (anonymous), 45-46
Weil, Simone, 49
Welch, John, 41